My Unboxed Heart

Breaking Free From the Bondages of an
Emotionally Abusive Mother

Kari L. Jones

My Unboxed Heart
© 2022 by Kari L. Jones
www.KariLJones.com

This title is also available in Kindle format.

ISBN: 979-8-9872994-0-1

Cover design by Krista Dunk, www.100XPublishing.com
Cover image by © Romolo Tavani, Dreamstime.com, used with license

My Unboxed Heart has beautifully unpacked the sometimes fearful and overwhelming baggage that the verbally and emotionally abused heart often carries. Kari L. Jones meticulously digs deep into unspoken areas of open and pushed-down wounds with raw honesty about God, herself, and the human soul. She guides the reader down a step-by-step path of recovery to God's intended heart alignment, with each chapter ending in an unpacked prayer. This book lays out a clear scriptural path toward healing that even the bloodiest of wounds can amend. I feel any woman who has faced verbal abuse or emotional wounding should have a copy of *My Unboxed Heart*. It is truly a book you can read again and again throughout the seasons of life.

— Barbara Holmes, author of *He Calls Me Bethany* and *Finding Rest in The Garden of The Lord*

In *My Unboxed Heart,* Kari shares her personal story in a real, raw and impactful way. If you want to make peace with yourself, God or someone who "plays mind games, manipulates, gaslights (makes you question your perception of reality), is passive aggressive, mocks, criticizes, and/or makes fun of you" then you need to read *My Unboxed Heart*. Or maybe you are asking yourself, "What has God put into me to fulfill?" Then you also need to read *My Unboxed Heart*. Sharing from a healed and free heart, Kari gives powerful testimony, steps, and scriptures of identity, love, hope, and authority that God has given her to bring healing and freedom so you can also operate from a place of healing and freedom with an unboxed heart.

— Krystal Travis, author of *Label Breaker: Finding Your Identity in a World of Labels*

Author Kari Jones has done a brave work with *My Unboxed Heart*. She shares her difficult experiences and journey, as well as her solutions and revelations from the Lord. Anyone who has experienced emotional abuse from a loved one will be blessed and have a clear path to healing their hearts and renewing their minds. Thank you, Kari, for writing about an important topic that's rarely discussed.

— Krista Dunk, author and director of 100X Publishing

One of the most complicated relationships a woman can have in her life is the one with her mom. It is supposed to be maternal. It is supposed to be caring. Your mother's arms are where you should be able to go for safety and comfort and security and yet many of us never get that opportunity. In *My Unboxed Heart*, Kari opens up in a beautifully vulnerable but strong way to take us on the journey of her walk with her mom, the pain that it caused and how she healed with the help of Jesus. This book will challenge you but also allow you to feel seen. To feel understood. It gives you a faith-based approach to heal. The strength Kari shows in this book is outstanding and I am in awe of her faith journey.

— Dawn Taylor, Trauma, Business and Life Coach,
author, and founder of The Taylor Way

To
My Best Friend, My Adventure Partner,
My Greatest Cheerleader, My Lover, My Man,
My Husband

Table of Contents

Message From The Author

This is an inspirational book to equip and empower women who feel paralyzed in life from deep, emotional maternal heart wounds. If this is you, after reading this book, you will walk away with what you need to either begin or continue your heart-healing journey and freedom to passionately live out the life you feel deep in your soul. I desire for women to know and understand they are not alone. Carrying around deep, emotional maternal heart wounds is more common than most of us think.

I truly believe it only takes one word, thoughtless or intentional, to do enough emotional damage to prevent us from living out our purpose to the fullest. The emotionally abused often suffer in silence, afraid to speak out because we have rationalized, since we were not physically or sexually abused, we weren't "abused" enough to matter. We are afraid no one will believe us or care enough to listen. The truth is, we do matter, our hearts matter and the purpose we were designed for matters.

I further believe every person has maternal heart wounds, whether small or great, and whether our mother was abusive or the most loving in the world. We live in a fallen world. Every mother is a part of that fallen world and has a sinful nature. In short, mothers are not perfect and can leave a wound in a vulnerable child's heart, intentional or not. It happens.

Sometimes we don't even know we have a maternal heart wound until an unexpected, epic deliverance session in our adult years. The important thing is to be intentional about working toward a completely healed heart. Why? So we can experience the abundant life we were designed for, enter into crazy intimacy with our Creator and gain full confidence in who we are made to be.

This book is an account of my personal journey and my experiences at the time of writing. I say at the time of writing, because

I believe healing may be a life-long journey. We can always go deeper with God and always learn more about who we were made to be. The layers of who we are in Him, I believe, go way deeper than any of us can imagine.

My story is my story; it is not anyone else's and it is not meant to be. Take what you want and leave the rest. I have written for inner healing purposes for my own life. It is not intended to hurt or harm anyone. My heart is for healing, freedom and fulfilling the powerful purposes each of us are designed to fulfill.

Kari L. Jones

Introduction

Identity Shift

I was sitting in the car completely heart broken and confused. There was so much tension in the air. My sister was whimpering in her car seat. I couldn't help but feel that every one of my mother's angry moves was directed at me, communicating that I was a disappointment. For the first time, I knew I would *never* please her.

My younger sister and I had joined my mother on a visit to one of her church friends. I was about six years old. My mother's friend had two children of her own, one my sister's age and a baby. Even though there were no children my age to play with, I do remember sitting on the floor in a bedroom playing with dolls with the younger girls. I don't remember many more details about the play time, but the incident that ended our play was etched into my mind as a clear memory, replayed for decades. For whatever reason, the other little girl hit my sister in the back. My sister started to cry loudly. I immediately got up and ran to get my mother. When I reached her, I told her that my sister had been hit by the other girl. She quickly went to my sister. I stood back and let my mother handle the situation.

As I stood there, I do remember having the thought *mom will be so proud of me for doing the right thing and getting an adult.* Like most children, I was taught to always get an adult in situations like this and to not handle it on my own. Despite all the times I previously didn't apply this rule, this time I had.

My mother was upset, and we prepared to leave. Putting on my shoes and heading to the car, I felt a sense of pride that I did the right thing. I knew that I hadn't always, but today, I did what Mother told me to.

When we were getting into the car, honestly, I was expecting a little praise, hoping to hear, "Kari, you did the right thing in there; you got an adult." My happy bubble was soon burst.

I watched my mother get into car. She put her seatbelt on, then put the keys in the ignition. Every motion was done in haste. I could see she was clenching her jaw; her eyebrows were narrowed. She was angry. Looking at her, waiting for my praise, she finally spoke, "You should have hit her back. You should have protected your sister." I was shocked. My pride bubble burst. I don't remember if I tried to defend myself, explaining that I just did what she taught me: I got an adult. I do remember feeling like she was angry with me for, once again, being a huge disappointment.

This moment has remained etched in my mind like a scar reminding me that whatever I do in life, whether it is exactly what she asks of me or not, I would never please her. This reality haunted me well into my adult years, however it did not remain painful. I found healing for this memory so that it no longer produces feelings of hurt, rejection and anger. Instead, I now feel warmth, grace and love. I learned the power of taking a painful memory to Jesus through prayer and asking, "Where were You?"

With this memory, Jesus took me back and allowed me to see myself sitting in the front seat of the car as a crushed little girl. Then, in a blink of an eye, I saw Jesus in the memory. I am sitting on His lap, He is holding me close, and I watched as He leaned over to whisper in my ear. I hear Jesus' gentle voice softly speak, "I am proud of you." With those words, all the hurt, anger and pain melted away from this memory and I instantly felt seen, acknowledged and loved.

My identity shifted from being the disappointing daughter of my mother to the proud, loved daughter of the King of Kings. Through my healing journey I experienced the all-consuming fire of God's love, burning up every offense in every memory, and I am now able to see or sense the presence of Jesus in each one.

ONE

The Lie, My Revelation

Hugging my legs close to my chest, I rocked back and forth in the fetal position on my bed, groaning through each wave of sharp, intense pain. I was soaking my bed sheets with sweat while begging God to relieve me from this torture. Occasionally I would scream into my pillow when the wave of pain, or contraction, was really intense. In a split second between the contractions, I found the energy to run to the bathroom to beat the uncontrollable flow of diarrhea.

Sitting on the toilet, a short time of relief came as I felt my body release the yuckiness. I leaned over, placed my crossed arms on my legs and allowed my head to rest on my arms. I took some really deep breathes knowing I would need to conserve my energy. Having been through this several times before, I knew I wasn't near finished. This short relief from the pain quickly ended as I found myself urgently switching from sitting to leaning over the toilet, puking. If only I could puke just the once, but no…the violent intervals had begun.

I tried to rest between each interval by lying on the bathroom floor in front of the toilet closing my eyes, trying to sleep. But sleep would not come before I found myself hugging the toilet again for the second, third, fourth and fifth time. When the dry heaving began, I knew I would soon be able to return to the comfort of my bed.

When my body told me it was done, the slow and strenuous journey back to my bed began. I was incredibly weak, feeling like I had just pooped out or threw up every ounce of energy I had in my body. I found myself crawling on the floor because trying to stand up made me feel dizzy. It took everything I had in me to stand just to slip into my bed and pull the covers over me. I promptly returned to the fetal position. Sharp, intense contractions of pain began again. Shaking from weakness and clutching my bed sheets as I groaned through each contraction is how I remained until, by the grace of God, I was able to fall asleep, leaving this world of pain, even if it was just for a short time.

Unfortunately, this was my monthly fate since the time I began my period at age 12. I would beg Mother for medicine or anything that could help, but did not receive the aid I needed. I feared there was something terribly wrong with me, however my mother assured me this was normal. "Some women just have it worse than others," she would say. I suffered monthly, convinced there was no relief and this was my lot in life. I felt I must be a really bad person for God to feel the need to punish me monthly. If He saw it fit, then I must deserve it.

One day during high school, after years of suffering, I was casually talking with some of my girlfriends about how terrible my monthly periods were and how much I hated them. One of my friends asked if I had gone to the doctor. I told her that my mom said this was normal and has refused my many requests to go to the doctor about this. Shocked, my friend shared that there was medicine and natural remedies that help with this and this suffering is not normal; there is help out there. WAIT, WHAT!?! Every one of my friends in this little gathering were agreeing; there was relief from my pain and I shouldn't be needlessly suffering. Some even shared they, too, use to have a hard time, but since visiting the doctor, found the remedies that worked for them and didn't have problems any more.

Full of hope, I went home that day, honestly thinking maybe my mom didn't know there was medicine out there that could help me. I was excited to share with her what I had learned from my school friends; there was help and I really wanted to see a doctor to start exploring my options for this physical problem. All of my excitement and hopes were squashed when, after excitedly sharing with my mother, she replied, "I know, you don't need that." Devastated, I ask, "Why?" She replied, "I suffered through and so can you."

Heartbroken, I went to my room feeling defeated. I couldn't believe it. My mom just identified with my pain and admitted that she was choosing to have me suffer anyway. In that moment I remember vowing that I would be a better mother than she was. I would not allow my daughter to suffer the way she was allowing me to.

Sometime later, after many more monthly sufferings, my younger sister who had recently been introduced to this wonderful monthly friend, was complaining to me about how much pain she had recently suffered through. I responded by sharing that she wasn't alone. I also suffer monthly and it really sucks. Not too long after that, I was in her room for a reason I do not remember. While I was in there, my eyes were drawn to some medication on her desk. I picked it up and asked her what this was for. She replied that it was for her monthly periods and it has helped tremendously. I asked how she got it and she replied that mom had taken her to the doctor to get medicine after she complained about the pain.

WHAT!? I was immediately angry. I had practically begged mom to take me to the doctor and she had refused. I confronted my mother about my sister's medicine, the medicine she had been denying me for years. I was angry and I wanted an answer. My mother replied, without showing any emotion, "She can't handle pain like you can." And that was that. My mother walked away without any other explanation. I said I wanted to go to the doctor too. "I want relief from this suffering too," but the answer was still, "No!"

Years later as an adult, this memory would stir up feelings of rejection, anger and bitterness and reinstate the lie I had partnered with and allowed to have free rein in my mind most of my childhood and young adult years: I wasn't worthy. However, I do not want to feel this way anymore. Focusing on the negativity of the memory was poison to my mental and physical health. It would set me on toxic thought merry-go-rounds preventing me from moving forward in my creativity, problem solving, learning and success. As a result, I brought the memory to Jesus and I asked, "Jesus, where were You?"

Holy Spirit then showed me a picture of Jesus standing right in front of me, arms open wide, saying, "Kari, let Me be Judge." Sadly, the noise of anger and offense was louder to me in that moment, and I didn't hear Jesus. I didn't see Jesus. All I saw was an offense and a need for justice. I had not yet understood Jesus as my righteous Judge. I had not yet understood that I didn't have to play the role of judge and that I could release my offense to Him.

As Holy Spirit led me through this memory, I felt so much love radiating from Him; He truly didn't want me to hurt. He genuinely wanted to take all my pain, but I was the block choosing to hang on to it rather than release it.

The big memory shifter, however, was that the love radiating off of Jesus wasn't only for me; I felt that it was for my mom too. Jesus didn't want her to hurt anymore either. Here we were, my mother and I, both hurting women, doing our best to protect our own hearts. We were both hanging on tightly to our anger and bitterness like a security blanket and both completely oblivious to the freedom and love being offered by the One who already took it all.

Then, I found myself looking at my mother and saying, "Mom, I am sorry you went through so much pain. You don't have to carry it any more. Let's both release it to Jesus." In this memory, I now feel love, compassion and value. The lie was exposed.

The Lie Hidden

The emotional abuse that came from my mother formed massive, deep wounds in my heart, paralyzing me from living the life I felt passionately about deep in my soul. I suffered with these heart wounds and was a victim, paralyzed by it for most of my life and didn't even know it. With my mother, I went years, even decades, without recognizing her treatment and behavior as abuse, and it took God intervening to reveal it to me. I had been living with an underlying anger, defeat, and pain.

Hating her, even though I didn't want to, had been a part of me for so long, I found myself asking if freedom from this depressing heaviness was even possible. I wondered if I had the boldness to take the steps necessary away from the familiar into the unknown. Would I risk it all for the hope of healing the deep maternal heart wounds and to experience life the way I craved? My relationship with Jesus was my hope that there was freedom and abundant joy at the end of this dark, claustrophobic tunnel. As long as Jesus remained my hope, I vowed I would never stop fighting for my emotional freedom. I wanted it more than anything else.

For most of my life I lived with the pain that there was something wrong with me. Interacting with my mother was confusing and frustrating. My father was there, but not there, if you know what I mean? His focus was on providing for the family. I didn't know where I fit in. Throughout childhood I was constantly trying to earn my mother's love and affection, which made me feel lost. Stepping back and allowing God to make sense of it all, I have come to recognize how much of my maternal emotional abuse distorted my perception of who I am, who God created me to be.

This quote from an article I read articulates exactly how I felt and gives reason for my reactions to my mother's emotional abuse: "Instead of being given the building blocks of a healthy self-esteem, we internalize a nagging inner critic and a perpetual sense of self-doubt"[1].

Reflecting on my childhood, I felt my mother made destructive comparisons among her children and my peers. In my perception, her comparisons taught me that I fell short in areas of personality, obedient behavior and ability to succeed. I felt she made my brother the golden child, adoring him excessively, supporting him in all his interests and activities, and coming to his rescue while leaving me to

---

[1] Walker, P. (2013). *Complex PTSD: From surviving to thriving*. Lafayette, CA: Azure Coyote.

fend for myself. I felt that my mother was devoted to his comfort, yet had zero empathy toward me. I felt my sister, who fell extremely ill as a baby, yet made a full recovery, was always treated like she was fragile, and very little was ever expected from her. My continued observations of what I perceived as comparisons left me believing there was something wrong with me.

This learned behavior continued into adulthood, and I compared myself with everyone. Looking for a way to elevate myself, the "inner nagging critic" would remind me of my place: undeserving of self-confidence. This led to devaluing myself and returning to the lonely, familiar emotional place of my wounded heart. The evidence kept mounting that *there must be something wrong with me.*

Now, being on the other side of the tunnel and freed from the emotional prison of my wounded heart I can confidently share I made the wrong conclusion about myself. There was nothing wrong with me. I had mistakenly concluded, *if I just figure out what is wrong with me, I can fix it and finally experience the joy-filled life I long for.* Unfortunately, since there was nothing wrong with me, my strategy for "fixing" myself wouldn't work.

My mother's inability to provide a healthy relationship, a safe and loving environment, tune into my emotions, acknowledge my pain, and meet my basic emotional developmental needs was not my fault, and I can't fix it! There was a hidden lie at work on the inside of me trying to destroy the core of my being.

The Lie At Work

The daily struggle to just breathe in a house that felt more like a prison is hard to put into words. It is hard to express the emotional strongholds formed during a childhood from a series of intangible events. I hesitated to seek help from others because in the past when I tried to verbalize the cause of my pain, it was too easily dismissed with a quick, "Maybe your mom was having a bad day." While inside I am screaming, *A bad day? Like, every day? Without ever having a conversation where apologies are given for the behavior initiated from a bad day?* Every time a person dismissed the pain I felt and ignored my cry for help, I went deeper within myself, and it became harder and harder to find the escape I so desperately needed.

Each day was filled with my mother's disappointing looks, her hurtful words, her controlling and manipulating behaviors, erratic shifts in emotions, her ever-conditional "love," and her constant shaming ways. All of it formed a persistent sense of anxiety, when I should have felt safe and secure. No matter what I did I couldn't fix this suffocating atmosphere.

I recall one instance during my immigration to the States. At the time I was living in Canada with my son, in my parents' house, while my husband was living in the United States, working to prove he could financially support his family. This was a requirement in order for us to be granted permanent resident visas.

During this time, I worked mornings teaching at a local middle and high school while my son played at a friend's home. Being a single mom and being separated from the love of my life led to feelings of loneliness and inadequacy, and isolation often overwhelmed me. The hope of someday being able to live together as a family, with my husband and son in the same country, that was often the only thing keeping me from having a breakdown.

After a three-month separation, my husband came to visit for a few days. I feel like there isn't a word created to describe how excited we were to spend some quality time together as a family. On one of his first few days in town, he picked me up from work and we chose to go do one of our favorite things to do together: take an off-road adventure. Knowing our visit was short, we were trying to savor every moment together.

Nearing the dinner hour, we decided to head back to my parents' place and check in, maybe spend dinner with them, as we knew they would be getting off work soon. We weren't sure how our evening would be spent, but as long as we were together, we were happy.

Our moments of bliss changed shortly after arriving. We entered the home, bringing our joyous reunion spirits in. Walking into the family room, we saw my brother, who was also living with my parents at this time, watching a movie. Dirty dishes and snack wrappers filled the area where he seemed to have spent the day, clearly enjoying his day off work. We greeted him and took a moment to check out what he was watching. A couple minutes later my mom got home from work.

My husband and I were still standing there in the family room. My mother walked in, and we pleasantly greeted each other. My brother didn't remove his eyes from the TV. My mother noticed the dirty dishes and wrappers and immediately started picking everything up.

As she's cleaning, she asks, "Kari, did you start dinner?" *What?* I think to myself, *of course I didn't, I just walked in myself.* I quickly explain that my husband and I had just arrived home ourselves and had not prepared anything. Nothing was previously communicated about dinner, and dinner was something I did not prepare regularly, at all. I was confused. Since my husband was there visiting, I assumed we would be free to make our own schedule and enjoy our short days together. I should have known better. We came home to check in and see what everyone else was doing. I should also add, this was my pre-cell phone days, so there was no texting or calling while we were out on our adventure.

Previously when my husband had been a guest in my mother's home she had a way of manipulating how we spent our time, causing some very sour experiences and tender conversations between my husband and I. I never understood why, but I often defended my mother. I thought I was "keeping the peace" by not resisting her desires. My eyes were soon opened.

After hearing that I hadn't started dinner, even though my mother never communicated with me to do so, she began to harshly verbalize her disapproval of me. She strongly felt, since she worked all day, the least I could have done was start dinner. During her lecture, I remember my mom pausing in the midst of her angry words, arms overflowing with dirty dishes and snack wrappers, she looks at my brother, completely changes her tone of voice, and pleasantly asks, "Did you enjoy your day off?" My brother grunts, indicating both *yes* and also *do not disturb me, I'm watching a movie*. Satisfied with the answer, my mother stands up, and begins to walk to the kitchen. Before fully leaving the room, she intentionally glares at me, a glare I am too familiar with, further communicating her disappointment.

I wanted to cry. In a moment, the joy of the reunion, the freedom to celebrate, the love of the gift, all melted away and was replaced by shame, guilt, anger and defeat. It was taken from me as if I didn't deserve to have it. My husband, who was standing next to me through the whole scene, turned to me and asks, "What just happened?" (Before you judge my husband for not defending me in that moment, please know I had begged him many times before, in similar situations, to just stay out of it. I was afraid he would make the situation worse. My husband was really just respecting my wishes.)

If this one moment in time was an isolated event resulting from a bad day had at work, it would have been cleared up with a conversation, recognizing the surrounding circumstances, apologies shared and forgiveness extended. However, this is an example of an environment I called home throughout my childhood and early adult years. This is an example of the daily experiences that shaped me, forming my mindset about who I was and how I was supposed to fit into this world.

The memory of this event remains engraved in my mind as a pivotal moment. In the few short years my husband had known my parents, he had witnessed my mother mistreat me, change her tone negatively when speaking to me, change her demeanor when addressing me, ridicule me, make fun of me, manipulate me, control me, and mislead me. No, it wasn't my imagination! I had been betrayed. That day, standing in the family room, feeling defeated and undeserving, became the moment when change started to happen.

With my husband standing beside me it was time to recognize and acknowledge the lie I carried around with me like a weighted blanket.

The Lie Exposed

The lie I had to recognize and acknowledge was: "I am undeserving, not enough, less than and worthless." I do believe there are many lies I have accepted during my experience as a victim of emotional abuse, but this one lie seems to be at the core of all the others. My mother's inability to provide a healthy relationship translated to me that I am undeserving of healthy relationships. My mother's inability to provide a safe and loving environment translated to me that I didn't deserve to live in a loving environment. My mother's inability to tune into my emotions translated to me that I don't deserve to be heard, and as a result, I must bottle everything inside. My mother's inability to acknowledge my pain and meet my basic emotional developmental needs translated to me that I didn't deserve to be confident in myself, I didn't deserve praise of any kind, I didn't deserve to be celebrated, I didn't deserve, nor was I worth the effort.

The truth is I *am* deserving, I am more than enough and I am WORTH it all. I know this because I truly believe Jesus Christ gave it all for me on the cross. When I read the Bible I intentionally personalize the scriptures to allow the truth of them to come alive in my spirit and so they soak deep into my heart and mind. Jesus gave Himself for me. Jesus gave up His family, His reputation, His popularity and His position for me. He gave it all so He can be in a healthy relationship with me FOREVER! He gave it all to give me a new life. The crappy, miserable life I had been experiencing is not the one I was intended to live. It is, however, a clear result of the evil one making sure I would never know my true identity and fulfill my purpose in advancing the Kingdom of YAHWEH, glorifying His name and drawing others closer to Him.

My mindset, which has shaped the way I see myself, has been rooted in my childhood, and this lie that I am undeserving, not enough, less than and worthless has been so cleverly hidden. Why? I believe the one who hates us finds pleasure in keeping all of us in the dark about our true identity. Through Jesus Christ and His work on the cross we are deserving, we are enough, we are more than and we are worth it. I had to acknowledge the lie in my own life to start seeing, feeling and experiencing the truth about who I truly am, who I was made to be.

Unseen Purpose

Being able to label the source of my ever "nagging inner critic" and anxiety as emotional abuse was the beginning of a series of breakthroughs that led to freedom and a joy-filled life. Emotional abuse is real. It is a thing. I am not alone, and there is nothing wrong with me. I didn't have to have bruises and scars as proof to believe I had been abused. The next breakthrough would come with defining what abuse is.

Abuse doesn't only come in the form of physical or sexual, as I previously had thought. Abuse comes in many different forms, some less obvious than others. Doing a quick search into the word abuse, I learned, "The word *abuse* is made up of two parts — "use," which means to employ, and ab-, a Latin prefix meaning "away" — and as a whole comes from the Latin *abūsus*, meaning "misuse," or "use wrongly" (www.vocabulary.com/dictionary/abuse).

To be abused is to be misused. Another way of looking at it is to say abuse is *abnormal use*. Abuse is NOT normal. That is why I was having this deep emotionally struggle. I was not being treated the way I was designed to be treated.

I believe strongly each and every one of us is created with a powerful purpose by a powerful God. We are designed with a purpose to advance His Kingdom, to draw others closer to Himself and to glorify His name. Our unique design is not matched by anyone else in the world. No one else in all the world has the same purpose I do. Now I understand I have been mistreated by my mother because she does not see the purpose God created me for. If you have been paralyzed in life by the wounds your mother caused due to her inability to see your full God-given purpose, there is healing from those wounds so that you can be mobilized to fulfill your purpose.

This revelation caused me to feel angry. It brought up some pain I didn't realize was even there. The pain had been a part of me so long, I didn't even know I needed freedom from it, or that there is freedom from this depressing heaviness. This heaviness caused by abuse is not normal and God says there is an end. There is freedom. I was tired of trying to figure this all out, but I was determined to find freedom.

If you have "undeserving" feelings creeping in, tell them NO! You deserve to be free. Freedom is yours if you want it. It is God's desire for you. Even if you feel like a terrible person all the way to your core (like I did), I want you to know God is greater than our worst. He takes the worst in us and weaves it into His story for the purpose of glorifying His name and drawing others to Him.

Listen To Wise Counsel

Growing up I could sense something wasn't right with my relationship with my mother. I knew this because I hated always feeling defeated around her. I felt I had to compete for her attention. I became angry with her for not accepting me for me. I never felt loved by her. Every time she said those words, "I love you," they felt so empty. As a child I hated hearing her say them because they were so meaningless. It felt as though they were said out of obligation or habit, like when you say, "Bye" at the end of a phone conversation. So much of my being hated her, yet so much more of me wanted her approval, acceptance and love. The emotional tug-of-war was destroying me from the inside out.

I hated feeling like there was something wrong with me. The

weight of my mother's disappointment and constant ridiculing was more than I could handle as it fed the war within. It was a never-ending tormenting battle between anger and hate toward her and the longing for that motherly love and security.

It was clear there was something wrong, but I could never pinpoint it. The only conclusion I had come to and believed was there was something wrong with me. This was a lie planted by the evil one, yet my Father in Heaven would not allow it to overtake me. He had a plan to rescue my heart.

A pivotal moment in my thinking occurred one Sunday after church. I was a teenager, standing in the foyer, off to the side against the wall, waiting for my mother to be done visiting so we could go home. I wasn't talking to anyone; I just stood there as I often did on Sundays. An older lady in the congregation approached me and said, "How does it make you feel?" I was first surprised she was talking to me, because she didn't normally, and then confused by the question. I replied, "Excuse me?" This older lady, repeated the question with more clarity, "How does it make you feel – the way your mother treats you?"

I was shocked by the question. For the first time in my memory, someone was acknowledging what I had been feeling. Not knowing how to answer, I just said, "I don't know." This elder churchgoer ended our little interaction by sharing that she "sees" me and has seen the way my mother treats me. I didn't speak to that woman much before and not much after this interaction. I know that it was for God's purpose she felt compelled to approach me that day.

From that Sunday forward God led people into my life to say things that acted as guide posts, directing me to the truth I needed to discover. For example, another time, another woman in another location, whom I also didn't know well, approached me and gave me a big hug. As she hugged me, she said, "I don't know why your mother doesn't love you." She hugged me a long time. And again, I was so taken back by her words. They cut deep to a heart wound I wasn't aware was visible. How did she know? She also shared that she had seen the way my mother treated me and it made her sad. At the end of the long hug, she told me I was so lovable.

Even after leaving for college more adults would come into my life at unexpected times, God-sent guideposts catching me off guard as each one shared their observations, which were very similar to each other. Throughout this whole time I didn't know what emotional abuse was. I had not heard about it. I couldn't give my mother's actions a name. Every time I reflected on my relationship with my mother I hated that there wasn't anything substantial to accuse her of. All my physical needs were met. She wasn't violent. She wasn't a drug addict or alcoholic. I wasn't molested or beaten. This made me feel so alone. How was I supposed to navigate through my deep heart wounds without being able to label what caused them? Finally deciding I needed help or else my inner emotional struggle would destroy me, I sought wise counsel.

I decided to go to a local church and request a meeting with the pastor. In this meeting, I shared about the tug-of war of emotions within me. I couldn't focus on anything, and it was affecting every relationship I had. I found myself living a hugely insecure life, but passionately wanting another. I shared that I didn't feel like myself, but didn't know how to be myself. I had to know if there was something wrong with me. The pastor assured me there wasn't anything wrong with me and recommended I begin counseling/a mentorship with an older woman in the church. He introduced us and we started meeting regularly.

During the first meeting I didn't want to hold back. I decided I would fully answer anything she asked. I wanted to be free from this emotional prison that was controlling my life. After being open with my life to my new mentor, she gave a life changing diagnosis. She said, "You have been emotionally abused." I didn't know how to process what she said because I wasn't aware that was even a thing. I asked for confirmation, "Is emotional abuse a real thing?" She assured me it was, and I was a victim of it. She began to educate me on emotional abuse and had more questions for me to answer. She would make statements about how emotional abusers operate and it truly sounded like she knew my mother even though they had never met.

I didn't jump on board right away. I went back to the pastor who recommended this mentor and shared what she had said. After hearing some of my story and asking questions about my mother, things she said, how she acted or reacted, he agreed with her. Later, I began some counseling from the pastor's wife, who also fully agreed with the diagnosis. I started to accept it and found the counseling helped tremendously. I wasn't feeling as alone as before. The counseling provided a safe place to talk about my feelings and sort them out in a healthy way. Before counseling, I had never learned how to sort out how I felt. I spent my whole life keeping my feelings inside, feeling like I didn't deserve to be heard.

After discovering I was being emotionally abused by my mother, I remember talking to a woman from my church back home whom I respected as a woman of God. Truly, I was seeking her opinion. Before I had even finished sharing what I had learned through counseling, she replied, "Absolutely!" Her response was another conformation. If that wasn't enough, I chose to Google "emotional abuse tests." I found one and decided to take it to see what it said. The result of the test revealed I was 100% being emotionally abused. I wasn't shocked because I had already had confirmation from multiple God-fearing adults – some who knew me as a child, some who had only known me in my adult years and some who didn't really know me at all. The result of the online test was what I needed to fully accept the truth and begin to take the necessary steps for healing my heart wounds.

Wise counsel helped me navigate through the fog caused by my raging emotions, clearly identify the root of my problem and see the truth so I could begin the journey of healing my heart. The war of emotions raging within me needed wise counsel. I could not win the emotional war without it. The Bible states in Proverbs 24:6 that it is necessary to have wise counsel in order to see the path to victory more clearly.

"Wise strategy is necessary to wage war,
and with many astute advisers
you'll see the path to victory more clearly."
Proverbs 24:6 (TPT)

My Mother Is Not My Enemy

A relationship with a mother is an important God-given instinct. It may be the most significant relationship, outside of Jesus, in shaping who we are. Our mother is someone who carried us inside of her and nurtured us from her own body. She is where we find security and self-esteem. I do believe our mothers are good and want what is best for their babies, yet they, too, are a product of a fallen world. Shaped themselves by lies, they are acting out of their own pain. As children we do not understand this and therefore find ourselves confused and frustrated as we interpret our daily experiences, whether they be good or bad.

Let me suggest that our mothers are not the enemy. I know the strong feelings and emotions we can battle within us toward her; I have felt them. There were nights when the feelings of hurt, anger and hate kept me awake. No matter how much my mother has hurt me, I now know she is not the true enemy, Satan is. He is the one who hates us and is out to kill, steal and destroy us.

My mother has been used as a vessel by Satan, also known as the devil and the accuser, to destroy me. Satan is not stupid. He has thousands of years of experience turning mothers against daughters, daughters against mothers, and keeping them from discovering who they really are, shutting down their ability to fulfill the powerful purpose they were designed for. Satan doesn't need to wipe me off the earth to fulfill his purpose. He just needs to keep me from fulfilling mine, and in return, use me as another one of his vessels keeping others from fulfilling theirs. It is a sick cycle that we all have

28

the power to break.

As a child, I was weak and in need of guidance, direction, correction, love, security, joy, peace, patience, and kindness to shape me. Due to sin in this world, I did not get everything I needed exactly in the way I was created to receive it. Yahweh is good. He still can use me to fulfill my purpose by allowing Him to father me, teach me, guide me, and love me. I believe my Heavenly Father, the King of Kings, Yahweh, is all I need. Before I discovered complete dependency on Yahweh, the devil met me as a child and took advantage of the knowledge he already had about me. The knowledge that I am created for a powerful purpose to glorify God, advance His Kingdom and draw others closer to Himself.

The evil one has constantly accused me, whispering in my ears and planting thoughts in my mind, making my character seem questionable and my efforts worthless. His weapon is getting me to believe, own and identify with the initial lie he implanted in me as a child, that I am undeserving, I will never be enough, I will always be less than and I am worthless. Satan's techniques have been well polished, as it has been used on generations before us. As a weak vulnerable child, I was the perfect target for a vicious enemy.

Learning and understanding the true enemy is Satan and my mother was his vessel, I was able to begin to shift my anger and hate from her to Satan. It also created a compassion for my mother I had never felt before. This compassion drove me to my knees to pray for her. I asked God to show me how He saw her, because I could not see her any other way than as my abuser, the one who crippled me from being who I was called to be. Every time a thought or memory came into my mind, stirring up the familiar anger, hate and pain, I trained myself to pray for my mother and recite scripture until those feelings went away.

God created me to have dominion, and I believe that includes over every thought, feeling and emotion. No one and nothing has my permission to dictate my emotions. Living in a state of anger and hate was not healthy. Feeling those emotions can be good, but then they have to be dealt with and released, not buried and festering. I heard someone say once, "Just because a thought comes into your mind, it doesn't mean you have to think it." I am the one who has been given control of me. One of the fruits of the spirit is self-control. If I am not going to practice self-control, then someone or something else will control me.

I prepared "emergency verses" from the Bible to help combat toxic thoughts or emotions that may arise within me, trying to get me to see my mother as the enemy. At the end of this chapter I have shared these Bible verses in case they are useful to you as well. Memorizing these verses make them quick to retrieve from memory when needed, which is a huge help. These Bible verses act as a sword against the weapons of the true enemy.

Taking Action

"In addition to all of these, hold up the shield of faith to stop the fiery arrows of the devil. Put on salvation as your helmet, and take the sword of the Spirit, which is the Word of God." Ephesians 6:16-17 (NLT)

I want to highlight two things in these verses. First, the devil has flaming arrows he throws at us. Our enemy, our true enemy, is relentless. We will have days we feel like the flaming arrows do not stop. The toxic thoughts running into our heads are like a waterfall drowning us. In these times is when we need to step out in faith, knowing this is the enemy trying to stop us from being and doing what we are called to be and do by our Creator God. In this verse it says, "hold up the shield of faith." This is a call to action. We want to stop those flaming arrows from hitting us and causing damage in our lives.

Each of us needs to know where our faith lies and walk in it. This means, if we truly believe the Bible is God's Word and it is absolutely true, then we will believe what it says about us, own these words as our identity and act and think on them as the model for our lives.

For example, God says I am loved. If there is a person who dares tells me or makes me feel like I am not lovable, I simply ignore that person as if they didn't say anything at all; I am not going to listen to words that contradict God's Word. I choose to take the action in believing I am created for the powerful purpose the Bible says I am. I will choose to hold up that shield of faith with boldness and confidence by believing what the Bible says about me. My mind, feelings and emotions are my dominion, and the devil is not welcome here.

The second thing I want you to pay attention to in Ephesians 6:16-17 is "take the sword of the Spirit, which is the Word of God." It is clear here God's Word, Bible verses, are a sword given to us to use against our enemy. This is why it is important to have some emergency verses ready to go the second a toxic thought enters our minds. I would encourage each of us to write these verses out, put them on our bathroom mirrors, have a voice memo on our phones with them we can listen to while driving and even make a song with them and sing them while we are doing the dishes or folding laundry. Putting songs to the verses is the best way I memorize scripture. I will boldly belt out my Bible verses to my made-up tunes in the car or at home, which sometimes annoys my kids. This is what it is to take action, so make it a point to memorize scriptures that will help you have healthy thoughts and a healthy mind. It also aids in maintaining an emotionally healthy life.

Emergency Verses

Feeling like mother is the enemy:

"For our struggle is not against flesh and blood, but against the
rulers, against the authorities, against the powers of this dark world
and against the spiritual forces of evil in the heavenly realms."
Ephesians 6:12 (NIV)

"Be well balanced and always alert, because your enemy, the devil, roams around incessantly, like a roaring lion looking for its prey to devour." 1 Peter 5:8 (TPT)

"Any kingdom that fights against itself will end up in ruins. And any family or community splintered by strife will fall apart." Matthew 12:25 (TPT)

Feeling angry:

"My dear brothers and sisters, take note of this: Everyone should be quick to listen, slow to speak and slow to become angry, because human anger does not produce the righteousness that God desires." James 1:19-20 (NIV)

"Don't sin by letting anger control you. Think about it overnight and remain silent." Psalm 4:4 (NLT)

"But I tell you, love your enemies and pray for those who persecute you," Matthew 5:44 (NIV)

"Do not take revenge, my dear friends, but leave room for God's wrath, for it is written: "It is mine to avenge; I will repay," says the Lord." Romans 12:19 (NIV)

"For I know the plans I have for you," declares the Lord, "plans to prosper you and not to harm you, plans to give you hope and a future." Jeremiah 29:11 (NIV)

Feeling defeated and alone:

"Be strong and courageous. Do not be afraid or terrified because of them, for the Lord your God goes with you; he will never leave you nor forsake you." Deuteronomy 31:6 (NIV)

"The Lord himself goes before you and will be with you; he will never leave you nor forsake you. Do not be afraid; do not be discouraged." Deuteronomy 31:8 (NIV)

Feeling worthless:

"We have become his poetry, a re-created people that will fulfill the destiny he has given each of us, for we are joined to Jesus, the Anointed One. Even before we were born, God planned in advance *our destiny* and the good works we would do *to fulfill it!*"
Ephesians 2:10 (TPT)

Feeling unheard:

For the eyes of the Lord are on the righteous
and his ears are attentive to their prayer,
but the face of the Lord is against those who do evil."
1 Peter 3:12 (NIV)

Unboxed Prayer

Dear Father,
You are my Creator and You created me with absolutely no mistakes. Your ways are perfect. I pray, Father, that You open my eyes to see every lie I have believed about myself. Lead me into Your truth. I want to see the fullness of my design. I want to believe, without a shadow of a doubt, that I am made for a powerful purpose and hold a unique calling. I want to walk in confidence in who I am in You and shake off every misunderstood conception other people had of me and those I have had of myself. I am Yours. Heal me from the inside out. Wash me with Your words so that the real me may be exposed. I desire to love all You made me to be.
In the mighty name of Yeshua, AMEN!

TWO

Forgiveness, My Weapon

I don't remember where I found it, but I found a bottle of gold glitter once when I was about six or seven years old. I loved how the gold glitter sparkled in the bottle – so shiny and beautiful. I don't know why, but I had what I thought was a brilliant idea to bless my mother. In my young mind, my amazing plan was to spread the gold glitter all over my mother's bed so that it would shine and sparkle. As I began to sprinkle the beautiful glitter all over her bed, I was role playing my mother's reaction in my head. "Oh! It is so beautiful!" I would imagine her saying. "My bed has never looked so magnificent, thank you!"

After emptying the whole bottle onto my mother's bed, I stood back to admire my work. Her bed shimmered; it was the most beautiful bed I had ever seen. Mistakenly I convinced myself that my mother would be proud and grateful. My imaginary praise evaporated when my mother walked into the room, gasped in horror and began disciplining me for my actions. She didn't love it. She hated it. She never commented on the beauty I saw, she just screamed her disappointment in me and how bad I had behaved.

I was crushed. I was confused. All I wanted to do was create something beautiful for my mother, and I wanted her to be proud of me. Neither happened. She didn't allow me to explain. My voice wasn't allowed to be heard. No questions were asked, just discipline given. I was angry with my mother for punishing me when my intention was just to please her. Why couldn't she see my heart? I was confused about the way she treated me, and I didn't want to forgive her. From the eyes of a little girl, I had done nothing wrong.

As an adult I understand my mother's reaction; I have absolutely no offense. She saw a huge mess and was probably very overwhelmed by it. Even though I know why she reacted that way, Holy Spirit brought this memory back to my mind to show me the moment when a wound was made in my little heart, where a seed of bitterness was planted and began to grow. I needed to revisit this memory and forgive my mother as part of my healing journey.

With my eyes closed, I asked Jesus, "Show me where You are in this memory." Almost immediately, I had a vision of myself as a little girl, my hands in the hands of Jesus, dancing in my mother's bedroom. We were enjoying the shine of the gold glitter spread all over the bed. "Isn't it beautiful?" I ask with pride in my voice. "Absolutely," Jesus replies, "It reminds me of Heaven." My heart is filled as I experience this memory with joy and I feel seen for the purity of my heart and my appreciation for beauty.

On another occasion when I was about nine years old my grandmother knit me a beautiful sweater. It was ivory and maroon, and I remember wearing it ice skating. I was always proud to wear my grandmother's sweaters. She made them with love, and I felt her love when I wore them.

One morning while I was proudly wearing it I accidentally spilled orange juice down the front of this gorgeous sweater. I quickly took it off and threw it into our dirty clothes pile in the hallway. When my mother came by and saw the sweater in the dirty clothes pile, she picked it up and threw it into my room. Seeing what she just did, I explained that I spilt orange juice down the front of it and it needed to be washed. She firmly told me that she wasn't going to wash the sweater. I began to plead my case, "But it has orange juice down the front of it. I can't wear it with orange juice on it." Even so, my mother stood firm and said she wouldn't wash it. "Sweaters like that can't be washed very often or they'll get ruined."

I understood what she was saying, but that didn't help my situation. "Okay, fine, then wash it this time and I will be more careful in the future." I was begging her to wash the sweater. If the sweater didn't get washed, I knew I wouldn't wear it and that made me sad. Not wearing it felt disrespectful toward my grandmother, but I didn't know what to do. She confirmed with me her final answer was no and made it clear that she'd better not find it in the dirty clothes again. Frustrated and angry I threw the sweater on the top shelf of my closet. I may have even shouted, "Fine, then I won't ever wear it again." On the top shelf on of my closet is where this sweater stayed for the next 15 years.

At age 18 I moved out, joined YWAM, moved back in, moved out again and went to college, moved back in, got married, and moved out, and all the while this orange juice-stained sweater remained on the top shelf of my childhood room's closet. When my husband and I were separated due to the immigration process, I moved back in with my parents. During this time I remembered the sweater and wondered if it was still up in the closet. I ventured into my old bedroom, opened the closet and looked up on the top shelf. To my surprise it was still there. Reaching up I grabbed the sweater, held it up and spread it out by the sleeves. I shook my head as I saw the orange juice still on the sweater 15 years later. *Incredible.*

I felt rebellious; the first thought that came into my mind was *wash it!* I ran down stairs to the laundry room and promptly threw the sweater into the washing machine. I set it on the gentle cycle and waited. Smiling to myself, I made this into a rebellious game in my mind. *If the sweater comes out ruined, mom wins. If the sweater comes out fine, I win.* If I won, I had one more reason why my anger and bitterness toward her was justified.

This was a sad thing. I was always justifying my anger toward my mom. I felt she deserved it. Generally, I was a really good kid, just not toward my mother. I didn't want to be good for her. She had squashed me too many times like a grape, unknowingly and uncaringly, and I could never figure out how to put myself back together. As a result, I justified choosing to be difficult for her.

I didn't respect her. I backed talked and didn't care about the consequences. When she yelled at me, that was my invitation to yell back at her. I was purposefully grumpy around her. At the dinner table I was forced to hold her hand during prayer. I would wipe my hand on my pants afterward as if she made my hand dirty. I would wish my parents would get a divorce just so I wouldn't have to live with her anymore. I would imagine my mother dying and vowed not to shed a tear at the funeral. She had hurt me so deeply, I wanted to hurt her too. What I didn't understand was by holding tightly onto my anger toward my mother for hurting me, I was actually really hurting myself. I needed to learn the power of forgiveness.

As for the sweater, it washed perfectly fine. No harm was done to it at all. Smelling the freshly laundered sweater I found myself grieving the loss of all the times I couldn't wear it. Since then it has been worn by my own daughters, but they haven't quite enjoyed it as I once had.

"Jesus, where were You in this memory of the sweater?" I ask, feeling sad that my younger self truly felt my attitude toward my mom was somehow protecting my aching heart that just wanted to be loved.

"I was right there, Kari, standing behind you. I was tapping on your shoulder. I wanted you to turn around and look at Me, not at your wounded heart. Your wounded heart blinded you to My love for so many years." As the Holy Spirit showed me a picture of Jesus trying to get my attention in the laundry room so many years ago, I see a tear roll down His cheek. "I don't want you to hurt any more, Kari." Jesus was genuinely moved to tears by His daughter's hurting heart. Many years passed after this moment, but I am so thankful I finally turned around, embraced the love of Jesus and experienced the power of forgiveness. I find myself saying, "I forgive my mother for the loss of time I had to wear the hand-knit sweater."

What Is Forgiveness?

Here is how Wikipedia defines forgiveness: "in a psychological sense, is the intentional and voluntary process by which one who may initially feel victimized, undergoes a change in feelings and attitude regarding a given offense, and overcomes negative emotions such as resentment and vengeance (however justified it might be)." From this definition, I understand forgiveness to be a conscious, deliberate choice to let go of my feelings and thoughts of resentment, bitterness, anger and revenge toward anyone who has hurt me, whether or not I feel they deserve it. Forgiveness is choosing to be willing to respond differently to an offense and give up my anger, even if I feel that I have the right to be angry. Forgiveness would be a decision on my part to no longer hold my offender accountable for the wrong they have done toward me.

I felt wronged by my mother. I felt mistreated by her. I felt my mother owed me. With each offense I chose to hang on to I was actually subconsciously keeping an internal record of her debt. This record of debt I carried around was heavy. The heavier it became the more resentment I built toward her. As time went on the chasm in our relationship widened as the debt became deeper. The resentment and anger grew stronger; she owed me! I did not want her to get away with what she had done to me. Angry and so hurt, I wanted my mother to pay back every penny of damage and loss she caused me.

Forgiveness would mean choosing to cancel my mother's debt without seeing any payment for this damage and loss. Forgiving my mother would mean I choose to stop fantasying about revenge. What did I do? I would choose to stop entertaining thoughts about bad things happening to her. I would choose to stop premeditating future come backs to her thoughtless hurtful words. I would choose and I have chosen.

I have chosen to release all the lingering anger toward her. I have chosen to let go of the heavy debt records. Resentment and bitterness toward her are gone. Mom, you are off the hook. You do not owe me. I forgive you. I forgive my mother.

Before we continue, I want to specify what forgiveness is *not*. The first time I felt the Lord calling me to forgive my mother, just the idea of forgiveness caused me emotional agony and gut-wrenching pain; I thought I was going to vomit or cry uncontrollably, unable to stop. Forgiveness was not easy. It wasn't easy because I thought it was minimizing the destructiveness of my mother's actions and the pain it caused. I have since learned forgiveness does **not** mean her behavior is excused. Also, forgiveness does **not** obligate me to rectify my relationship with her. Forgiveness was always *for me*. The power of forgiveness released me from my mother's emotional strongholds. Forgiveness brought peace to my mind, body and soul. Forgiveness enabled me to heal and released me to be the powerful Kingdom Citizen, Child of God, I am created to be. Ultimately, forgiveness is a weapon God uses to bring great victories over Satan, the evil one, and his destructive plans.

Why Is Forgiveness Necessary?

First, forgiveness is essential to experience deep joy and the abundant life God has promised (John 10:10). Second, as revealed in His Word, unless I learn to freely and wholly forgive and release all those who have offended and hurt me, I cannot expect my Father in Heaven to forgive me (Mark 11:24-26). And third, forgiveness is foundational to the healing process: emotionally, mentally, spiritually and physically. I believe holding on to unforgiveness and the anger and bitterness that goes along with it, is self-destructive and can make us physically and mentally sick. Even Henry Maudsley (1835-1918), a pioneering English psychiatrist, recognized that if we do not allow ourselves to grieve our losses, it can affect other parts of our being in a negative way. "The sorrow which has no vent in tears may make other organs weep."

Why Is Forgiving So Hard?

In my own experience, forgiving my mother was one of the hardest things I have ever done. It was an extremely painful journey, yet has come with great rewards, and I am trusting the greater reward is yet to come. When I first felt the Lord urge me to forgive my mother my initial reaction was, "NO!" I felt extending forgiveness to her would dismiss my pain, excuse my mother's behavior and put her in the right, leaving me to suffer in my pain for the rest of my life. I struggled with what God was asking me to do. *Why should I extend forgiveness to someone who isn't asking for it?*

Not only was she not asking for it, she didn't even recognize her continuous destructive behaviors were wrong. Yet, I was done with the inner suffering. I was craving freedom from all the shame, the guilt, the anger and the pain. I wanted the freedom so bad, I had to trust what God was asking me to do more than my feelings. I had to tell myself *feelings may be real, but they are not always the truth.* Forgiveness is a choice, and I made the conscious choice to forgive my mother.

Early on in my adulthood I recall a time when I decided to confront my mother on some recent behaviors that were hurting me. Talking to my mother about anything, other than weather, was extremely difficult. She had this way about her that always made me feel like the size of a peanut in her presence. She had to maintain the control at all times.

Throughout my life whenever I attempted to initiate a deep conversation I experienced an array of tactics: gaslighting, criticizing, blaming, and other subconscious ways of reminding that her place of great power above me would not be shaken, especially by me. As a result, I learned to have defenses up and ready every time we spoke. Her tactic of choice was not easy to predict, some were more forceful and damaging than others. Her mood always played a huge part for any conversation. The need for multiple defense modes became clear, and I trained myself to be able to quickly move from one defense mode to another, if necessary.

This continued well into my adult years. Consequently, leading up to this confrontation, I had to give myself many pep-talks to muster up the courage and meditate on the possible defenses I should have ready.

When I finally had enough courage I approached my mother and shared my heart with her about how certain behaviors were very hurtful to me. Hanging onto the hope that my heart felt expression would initiate a healthy conversation and would begin to change our relationship for the better, I was devastated when her response was, and I quote, "I feel I have done nothing wrong," and then proceeded to walk away. I felt that she just carved her answer into my heart with a sharp knife and left me to bleed out on a cold damp floor. Extending forgiveness to my mother was so hard; I had to come to terms with the fact that I was releasing her of a massive debt she may never even acknowledge she had. In other words, I had to forgive and be okay with never getting an apology. I had to choose to extend forgiveness without her asking for it or acknowledging anything.

This kind of forgiveness came with a grieving process. I had to grieve the loss of my hope for a healthy mother/daughter relationship. I had to grieve the loss of a repentance I may never see. I had to grieve the loss of the moment I had visualized in my head where my pain was acknowledged, forgiveness was requested and I would freely give it. I had to grieve the loss of a safe and loving home environment. I had to grieve the loss of mutual forgiveness between my mother and I. I had to grieve the loss of expectations, such as the expectation of my mother loving me, wanting me, valuing me. I had to grieve the loss of the ideal image of a mother I had created in my head. I grieved.

What I felt my mother owed me, I released to God. I had cancelled the debt, but at the same time I needed to give the paperwork, the debt records to someone. I recognized I could not just release it into the air, to the unknown. It would find its way back to haunt me in my moments of vulnerability. I decided to release it to the One who is tangible and could do something with it. The only One who can truly take an impossible debt and set us free is my Heavenly Father, my Abba, Yahweh! He is the One who knows the system of debts better than any other being, and therefore my trust is completely in

Him and His Word. God is the One. I passed the records of every owed debt to Him. I passed off every expectation to Him.

That day I literally found myself writing out all of the things I felt my mother owed me. About half way down the page my mind went blank. There was nothing else there. I couldn't think of another single offense, and yet at one point I thought I could write a list a mile long. I didn't know what happened, but then I heard the gentle whisper of my Heavenly Father say, "What does she owe you?" And I found myself replying, "Nothing."

I tore up the paper I had been writing on, held the pieces up like I was handing them to God and said, "It is all yours, Abba, she owes me nothing." Then I tossed the torn-up paper in the garbage.

Sometimes when I think about my loss and allow myself to grieve as I release the debt to my Heavenly Father I cry, sometimes I shout, but this time I was silent. Sometimes I am on my knees with my arms raised in the air. Sometimes I am lying on the ground, sometimes I pace the floor; this time I just sat.

I now see that when God was asking me to forgive my mother, He wasn't asking me to excuse the behavior. He was asking me to make the conscious choice to completely trust Him with the debt I thought she owed me so He could fully heal me. My God is gentle and reminds me, as His child and a citizen of His Kingdom, it is not my place to force justice where, when and how I see fit. Being a part of His Kingdom is acknowledging that He is King and trusting He will take care of all the injustice done to me, His child, in His perfect way and in His perfect timing.

"Never pay back evil with more evil.
Do things in such a way that everyone can see you are honorable.
Do all that you can to live in peace with everyone.
Dear friends, never take revenge. Leave that to the righteous anger of God. For the Scriptures say,
"I will take revenge; I will pay them back," says the Lord."
Romans 12:17-19 (NLT)

In this scripture God revealed to me the most important thing needed to rise above the abuse from my mother, and really any mistreatment I encounter from anyone in this life. By acknowledging God's Word to be true, I understand if I commit myself to Him, my Heavenly Father and my King, He promises to make things right on my behalf. He takes the responsibility to see justice done and debts paid. God sees me and the suffering my mother caused me. He promises in His Word that He will take care of it. It is my job to release my mother and all those who have hurt me to Him; I leave them with Him for Him to take care of.

Here are some more scriptures to support this call to action:

"Don't say, 'I will get even for this wrong.'
Wait for the Lord to handle the matter."
Proverbs 20:22 (NLT)

"And don't say, 'Now I can pay them back for what they've done to me!
I'll get even with them!'"
Proverbs 24:29 (NLT)

"For we know the one who said,
'I will take revenge.
I will pay them back.'"
Hebrews 10:30 (NLT)

Forgiveness Is A Process

Forgiving my mom has been a process. At one point it felt, no matter whether I forgave her or didn't forgive her, she still had the power to pull me back onto her merry-go-round, fueled by her mind games and hurtful words. I would try so hard to keep a smile on my face and ignore the mistreatment. Her behavior was exhausting. She would slowly strip me down layer by layer until I was so vulnerable it only took one word or look from her, and I would regretfully explode; using my own angry words as fiery darts aimed at her for destruction.

Ironically, my defensive reaction to my mom's inappropriate behavior was also inappropriate. I gave in and accepted her non-verbal invitation to dance – the dance of two people acting inappropriately with no harmony in sight. My passion for justice was not executed effectively. Fighting for myself the only way I knew how; I would not let her take me down without giving her a good fight. I had a lot to learn about fighting God's way.

Regret always followed when I defended myself against my mother. It never ended well and never in my favor. It felt like she took my defense as an invitation to shift her tactics to verbal abuse. I couldn't win. These exhausting dances left me feeling stuck, even though I felt like I was trying so hard to walk out forgiveness. *Did she even notice I was trying to live peacefully and not react? Why does it seem like she takes pleasure in pushing me until I break?*

It felt so intentional, as if it were some kind of sport for her. I would always beat myself up wondering, *why do I let her get to me? If I have forgiven her, why is it so hard to just ignore her?* Crying out to God for strength and wisdom in this relationship consumed my prayer life. *I must be forgiving wrong, or thinking I am forgiving but really not.* I was confused.

Honestly, in part, I was right in thinking I was forgiving wrong. I truly didn't understand forgiveness. Maybe that is why forgiveness has been such a journey for me. Forgiveness was not taught, practiced or modeled in my family. As a result, I had a misconception of what forgiveness really was and how to truly walk it out. I was figuring it out as I went. The one thing I was doing right was seeking help in the right place: on my knees at the feet of my Heavenly Father.

One day during the Christmas holidays I found myself wandering through the Christian book store looking for guidance from the Lord. I was home from college, just for the holidays, and my mother's behavior was more than I could handle. The mind games, the deception, the manipulating, the controlling had really felt like she had upped her game since the last time I saw her, or maybe she was making up for lost time? Whichever it was, I found myself in this book store needing help. I came across the shelf with the title "Forgiveness." *There are books on forgiving?* I thought to myself. I grabbed two, filled with the hope that I may find my answer in one of these books. I purchased them and began to read.

Early in the first book I read about asking for forgiveness from the one who mistreats you. This was a new concept. This new idea brought so many mixed feelings. I began to ask God if this is what He wanted me to do. I believed that any inappropriate behavior on my part was in reaction to my mom's inappropriate behavior. That may be true, but God started to work in my heart about taking ownership of my behavior.

It was not my fault my mother was emotionally abusive. I didn't ask for it, and even if I did it still wouldn't have been my fault because each person is responsible for their own behavior. My mother is a grown woman and knows what is right and what is wrong. So even if she was asked to engage in wrong behavior she has the choice not to! My mother is responsible for her actions, and I am responsible for mine. In the Kingdom of God self-control is one of the fruits of the Spirit. If the fruit of self-control is not visible in my life it is time for some self-reflection and self-correction.

Taking ownership of my behavior was a reflection of me. I had to wrap my mind and heart around what God was saying. At first I revisited all the feelings surrounding asking my mother for forgiveness; was I just excusing her behavior? It was like I had returned to a mountain I already conquered. Inner struggle began again, and I found myself arguing with God. *How could I ask my mother to forgive me when it was her behavior that provoked mine?*

"Never pay back evil with more evil. Do things in such a way that everyone can see you are honorable."
Romans 12:17 (NLT)

God was capturing my heart. He revealed to me that I was using my mother's behavior to justify my own. I knew I was not always in the right. I will be the first to say I'm not perfect. I threw fits of rage. I said hurtful words. I acted in destructive ways too. Surprise, surprise, I am a sinner. I can admit my own wrong behavior and also recognize when it is time for a change.

God was calling me to take ownership of my behaviors and it was a crossroads in my forgiveness journey. I had a choice to make: ignore what God was asking me to do and miss out on what He was going to do through this, or choose to be obedient, as uncomfortable as it was, trusting God for whatever plans He had. The spiritual growing pains were coming on strong.

The relationship with my mother, again, consumed my prayer life. How to go about this, I didn't know. The whole idea of trying to talk to my mother again about anything related to our relationship was making me physically ill. One day I decided to write down everything on paper. I asked God to bring to mind any and all behaviors I needed to repent of. I wrote them down and spent time confessing these things to God and repenting. In the future I didn't want to react inappropriately when I felt mistreated in any setting.

My heart poured out in a letter to my mom, asking her to forgive me of all my offensive behavior, whether it was known to me or not. It was an emotionally tough letter to write. Taking ownership of my behavior and asking forgiveness was what needed to happen.

The letter was delivered. During this time I hung on to the hope that maybe this was what God would use to create a healthy mother/daughter relationship. The little girl inside of me still wanted to be loved and valued by her mom. The results, however, were again crushing. She read the letter, left the letter and never said a word, not one, not ever.

Again, confused and frustrated, I found myself hurt and emotional at the feet of my Heavenly Father. *I did what You told me. So why...?* It took me years to understand I was hurt because I was hanging on to an expectation that I put on my mother to repay the debt I felt she owed me. I mistakenly thought my obedience to God, by asking her to forgive me of all my wrong behaviors toward her and under her, would soften her heart. It did not. What I did learn was obedience in giving it all to Him and allowing Him to be God, my debt collector, my protector, and my loving Father.

He, like a loving Father does, was teaching me a lesson I didn't even notice at the time. He wanted to have all of me. This obedience was about His relationship with *me*. He couldn't have all of me if I was hanging on to my mother so tightly. I had to let her go, all of her, every idea and hope of a relationship with her.

In addition to forgiving my mother and asking her to forgive me I also had to learn to forgive myself. I didn't ask for any of this. I didn't ask to be born, I didn't ask to have an emotionally abusive mother and I didn't ask to be devalued, hurt and ashamed. I didn't ask, but here I am and I have a choice. Do I let the devil win as I allow other people to determine my worth, or do I release it ALL to the One who made me, the One who did ask for me to be born because He has a powerful purpose for my life in His Kingdom. My past is not my fault, but what I decide to do with what I have been given is.

Choices

In relationship with my mother, here were my choices, as I saw them:

1) Remain having unrealistic expectations of her to complete me, which would result in never experiencing life with a healed heart and therefore never fulfill the purpose for which I was created.

2) Lower my expectations, and when I find myself offended by her stupid behavior, recognize that I may have given her too much credit as a human being and simply react by lowering my expectations, yet again.

3) Eliminate *all* expectations I have of my mother and completely give all of my expectations to God, therefore having zero expectations of her.

I didn't have to have a huge revelation to know God has called me to option 3: releasing all expectations to Him. By choosing to have zero expectations of my mother, I can't be offended.

Think about it, if you don't have any expectations of a person, and that person says or does something stupid, immature or potentially offensive, you didn't expect anything of them anyway, so it doesn't affect you. Also, walking away and choosing not to participate or engage in the stupid, inappropriate behavior is so much easier. On the flip side of that, I am in a position to be pleasantly surprised by any mature, responsible and encouraging behavior. Either way, I am not rattled off course or emotionally set back. I have learned to guard myself so I can be most effective for the Kingdom of Yahweh.

After forgiving my mom and forgiving myself, I forgave God. I know God does not sin and He does not make mistakes, however, somewhere in my subconscious I held a grudge against Him. I was angry at Him for giving me the mother that He did. I felt He could have given me a kind, loving and supportive mother, but He didn't. Why? I do not know. Forgiving God meant I let go of the offense that *He messed up in His choice of a mother for me.*

I know He is never wrong. His ways are higher than my ways (Isaiah 55:8-9). The Lord reminded me about Joseph. He was rejected by his brothers to the point of being sold into slavery, a far greater rejection than I have ever experienced. Joseph could have also questioned God's choice of family for him. Even so, God knew what He was doing. Many years later God used Joseph to save the family that rejected him from death by starvation, and in that, saved Yahweh's people. There is no way Joseph could have known the amazing outcome of his story, just as I also do not know the full outcome of mine.

I have faith in God there is a reason He gave me the mother I have, and I trust it is a far greater reason than I could ever imagine. What I do know is He will use my story to glorify His name. (You can read about Joseph's story in Genesis 37-43.)

Speak A Blessing

The last part of learning how to forgive is speaking a blessing over the people who hurt and offend me. In this case I chose to speak out loud a blessing over my mother. Believe me, the first time I did this was awkward and weird. I kept it short and sweet. With practice it has become part of my daily prayer for my mother. The Bible says,

"Your words are so powerful
that they will kill or give life,
and the talkative person will reap the consequences."
Proverbs 18:21 (TPT)

Many of my words previously had been speaking curses and death over my mother, and the results certainly haven't been in my favor. It was time to take responsibility for my words and speak life and blessing over her. My prayer is that my mother has a power encounter with the Holy Spirit where the tangible love of our Heavenly Father is so undeniable, she will be freed from her own emotional bondage and filled with life, the abundant life she was created for. May my mother be richly blessed.

Forgiveness is a journey. As I walk out forgiveness God continues to reveal new layers and fresh perspectives. There are always new levels of growth. In the beginning my heart was too hard from the pain to fully understand what I understand now about forgiveness. The Steps of Forgiveness/Loss found in Mary Leonard's book, *Ministering in Crises*, continues to be a helpful guide for me, and I highly recommend the read. My greatest benefit from my forgiveness journey has been the increased intimacy with God and the motivation to be obedient in whatever He asks me to do. Forgiveness has truly become a powerful weapon in obtaining and maintaining the abundant life I am created to live, with wholly healthy emotions, mind, spirit and body.

My Blessing to my mother:

Mom, I bless you. You are precious to me. I would not be who I am without you. I bless the day you were born and the day you were conceived. Angels rejoiced at your life. You were made for a powerful purpose, and I bless that purpose. You are a blessing to me and to the world. You are beautiful and you are one of a kind. There would be a hole in this world without you. You have a destiny to fulfill, and I bless that destiny. I bless all the things God designed you for. I bless every expression of who God made you to be.

Steps Of Forgiveness

1) Acknowledge an offense has been made, and take an account.
2) Accept the loss
3) Release the debt and exchange the pain for healing
4) Choose to cancel the debt, everything we feel owed to us
5) Release the offender to Jesus, who is the righteous judge, and speak a blessing over them.
6) Know that you have permission to speak forgiveness as many times as needed for the same offense. It could be 30+ times in the same prayer, and that is okay.

Unboxed Prayer

Dear Father,
Thank you for forgiving me of all of my sins. Please help me to forgive my mother and all those who have sinned against me and hurt me. I do not want to carry around anger, bitterness, offense and resentment for my mother or anyone else anymore. Show me how You feel about my mother. Show me how You feel about every person who has hurt me. I want to see them as You see them. Is there something You could tell me about my mother that would help me forgive her? Sharpen my ears to hear what You are saying. Help me

understand how she got to the point of hurting me. Fill my heart with Your love, that I may not sin against You and repeat to others the actions that caused pain to me.

In the mighty name of Yeshua, AMEN!

· THREE ·

Repentance, My Super Power

While rummaging through a box in my basement recently, I found an old journal from my high school years. Out of curiosity I started to read it. As I read I noticed how frequently I referred to myself as *selfish*. It didn't strike me as odd the first time I read it or even the second, but it definitely stood out when multiple entries in a row said it. Then I began to flip through the journal more quickly, wondering if this was a theme throughout the entire book. My suspicion was quickly confirmed. Over and over again I read sentences such as, "I am so selfish," "If I wasn't so selfish...," "Why am I so selfish?" *Why was I writing like this?* I thought to myself. I was truly shocked. This wasn't me.

In this moment, as if this were a divine appointment, God showed up and began to download an incredible map of my life and how this stronghold called "selfish" has hindered my growth as a person, preventing me from walking out the Kingdom the way I was designed to walk it out. This stronghold of "selfish" in my life was a pattern of thinking I had developed which dominated how I responded to people and circumstances around me. This pattern of thinking was not healthy. God began to do a work in my heart and my mind to make healthy patterns of thinking.

Selfish...I hated that word. It was not only a stronghold, but it was a trigger word, a word that would prompt involuntary memories of the traumatic experience of being called "selfish" repeatedly by my mother. Yes, it was traumatic because each time that word was used it was marked by a sense of helplessness and hurt. Even when my mother wasn't around, there were many days when her voice was on repeat in my mind. *You are so selfish. Quit being so selfish.* I always thought I didn't believe her. I saw myself as strong and a person of thick skin. I was determined not to allow my mother to upset me, hurt me or break me. Despite my determination I repeatedly failed at this mission, even into my adult years.

Staring at my journal, I hadn't realized the word *selfish* actually had such a deep effect on who I was, how I saw myself and how I responded to the world around me. Until this moment, sitting on my basement floor, in disbelief, I honestly had no idea the power of my mother's words. It was clear by the time I was a teenager I had accepted selfish as part of my identity. I owned it, and I didn't even know it. My mother had ingrained it into my being so well that she had me sabotaging myself, and here was the proof: my high school journal.

Selfish rung in my head so often with my mother's voice I wondered when it became my own voice. When did I buy it, believe it and identify myself with it? The most shocking part was I didn't even realize I had done it. I do not have a memory of consciously deciding my mother was correct. When did that happen? I know to my core this isn't me. Yes, I know by default of being part of the fallen human race we all have moments or times of selfishness, but this isn't our identity. This isn't who God created us to be. As a child of the Highest King my identity lies in Him not in selfishness.

In this moment the power of my mother's words became so real. I not only owned the identity of being selfish in my subconscious, but God was revealing to me the impact of this false identity in my adulthood and how it is connected to my place of feeling paralyzed and stuck. Because the word selfish was spoken over me again and again and again many of my life's decisions became a cry to prove I *wasn't* selfish.

Reflecting on my adult years, God was showing me how time and time again I would rearrange my schedule to help others. If someone were to call asking for help, even if I had other plans, I would cancel my plans to help. I was often the first to volunteer even when it was highly inconvenient. When I saw a need I felt it was my responsibility to fulfill that need somehow. I would put my own agenda aside, even my own family, to assist others. I lacked boundaries, because I misunderstood them as being *selfish*. I had become a rescuer which was hindering my own growth as a person. So many things have prevented me from moving forward in my life because I was busy proving to the world my mother was wrong; I wasn't selfish.

While rescuing everyone else I had ignored myself. To give this a visual, whenever I travel on an airplane a flight attendant gives pre-flight instructions. During these pre-flight instructions I have always heard them say something along the lines of, "In the case of a change in cabin pressure, an oxygen mask will drop in front of you from above. Please be sure to place the oxygen mask over your own face first before assisting anyone else, even your own children." They need to say this because this instruction goes against most parents' instincts. It is important to understand following this instruction is vital in an emergency, because if you pass out before your children you will not be able to assist them in whatever comes next. Not only will you not be able to assist your own children but also anyone else who may need your help, such as the elderly or disabled.

In the same way, being a rescuer to prove I wasn't selfish was like me running around the plane making sure everyone has their masks on before I put on my own. Afterward I would find myself gasping for air on the floor, unable to go on, crying out to God. He replied, "You feel so exhausted and paralyzed because you have ignored yourself in the decisions you have made up to this point. I cannot use you if you are not going to listen to My instruction. Your decisions from day to day throughout your adult years have been rooted in a heart wound that was caused by your mother. Selfish is not who you are."

My mother labeled me as selfish and I wore that label while trying to prove to myself and everyone else the label was wrong. I wanted the voice in my head to stop, and I didn't want any outside voices agreeing with it.

This revelation of myself was life changing. It was time to tear the label off and replace it with a new one that spoke truth and life over me. In order to do this I needed to repent, for not only accepting the lie that I was selfish, but for identifying myself with it and allowing it to dictate my day-to-day decisions as an adult. I am not selfish. I am child of the Highest King.

Caring for myself first means I am allowed to say no sometimes. I don't have to help every person who asks. I needed to learn how to say no, because I didn't know how. I spent my whole life saying yes, and until this revelation in my basement I didn't understand why it was so difficult for me to refuse. Saying no has always been a struggle, and now I understand why. I am not saying I shouldn't help at all; I just needed to learn how and when to say no – a lesson I was never taught. I was only taught I was selfish.

Why did God come to me in the basement and revealed this? Because He wants to set me free and heal me of this heart wound. He wants my heart to be fully alive and completely healthy. He is for me. Sitting on the basement floor, in response to the Spirit of the Lord, I prayed a prayer of repentance.

What Is Repentance?

According to Wikipedia repentance is "reviewing one's actions and feeling **contrition** or regret for past wrongs, which is accompanied by commitment to and actual actions that show and prove a change for the better. In modern times, it is generally seen as involving a commitment to personal change and the resolve to live a more responsible and humane life." In other words, repentance involves the commitment to change our heart (the way we feel), our mind (the way we think) and direction (the way we respond). It is like doing a little house cleaning and committing to keep it clean by choosing to change our everyday habits. Using the house as an analogy we can forgive the person who messed up our house, but repentance is choosing to clean it out and keep it clean.

In the Old Testament repenting was described as turning away from sin and turning toward God. Below is an example from Ezekiel. Other examples can be found Ezekiel 18:30; 33:11, Isaiah 45:22; 55:7 and Joel 2:12-13.

"Therefore, tell the people of Israel, 'This is what the Sovereign Lord says: Repent and turn away from your idols, and stop all your detestable sins.'" Ezekiel 14:6 (NLT)

The choice to repent shows a personal awareness that we are stained with sin and in need of cleansing. Sin is when we refuse to do the will of God, whether conscious or subconscious, according to His Word and His Spirit. In my life I had subconsciously adopted a wrong pattern of thinking. This pattern of thinking was not healthy for me and it was not the pattern of thinking I should have been operating with. It was not God's will. Once I was aware of this wrong pattern of thinking I chose to repent of it, turn away from it and replace it with a healthy pattern of thinking. This new pattern is built from the truth and is in alignment with the will of God for me according to His Word and Spirit. It has helped me to grow as a healthy human being, unstuck from the rut of wrong thinking. If I allowed myself to continue thinking I was selfish I wouldn't be able to break the exhausting pattern of proving myself to the world and wouldn't be able to experience my abundant joy filled life.

Thinking patterns include beliefs I have about who I am. My old thinking pattern believed I was a selfish person. My new thinking pattern is I believe I am complete and no longer have to prove myself to anyone,

"And our own completeness is now found in him. We are completely filled *with God* as Christ's fullness overflows within us. He is the Head of every kingdom and authority in the universe!" Colossians 2:10 (TPT)

Why Is Repentance Necessary?

Repentance is necessary because God said it is in His Word.

"The Lord does not delay [as though He were unable to act] *and* is not slow about His promise, as some count slowness, but is [extraordinarily] patient toward you, not wishing for any to perish but for all to come to repentance." 2 Peter 3:9 (AMP)

"From that time on Jesus began to proclaim his message with these words: 'Keep turning away from your sins and come back to God, for heaven's kingdom realm is now accessible.'" Matthew 4:17 (TPT)

"In the past God tolerated our ignorance of these things, but now the time of deception has passed away. He commands us all to repent and turn to God." Acts 17:30 (TPT)

Repentance, as said above, is changing the way we think, feel and respond to the world around us. It is necessary to exchange our incorrect thinking patterns for patterns built on truth in order for us to heal from our past and move toward a healthy future. Jesus, when He was here on earth, proclaimed the need for everyone to change the way they think. We need to change our minds about how we used to live life. John the Baptist also talked about the role of repentance when He said, "You must prove your repentance by a changed life" Matthew 3:8 (TPT). When we change the way we think we will live differently.

When God created humans in the beginning He created us with a powerful purpose:

"Then God blessed them, and God said to them, 'Be fruitful and multiply; fill the earth and subdue it; have dominion over the fish of the sea, over the birds of the air, and over every living thing that moves on the earth.'" Genesis 1:28 (NKJV)

I would like to highlight, "God said to them ... have dominion..." Did you catch that? God said to **them** - the 'them' is referring to humans, us. God did not say, "Let us have dominion." No, dominion was given to the human race to have over the earth. The second thing we have to understand is a human is a spirit being in an earthly body. Genesis 1:27 says God created male and female, but it wasn't until Genesis 2 when we read that God made the earthly body for the spirit of man to dwell in.

"And the Lord God formed man *of* the dust of the ground, and breathed into his nostrils the breath of life; and man became a living being." Genesis 2:7 (NKJV)

How do we communicate with God? We have spiritual experiences through our spirit. If you have never thought of yourself as having a spirit, then here are a couple other scriptures from the Bible referring to us as spiritual beings.

"After all, who can really see into a person's heart and know his hidden impulses except for that person's spirit? So, it is with God. His thoughts and secrets are only fully understood by his Spirit, the Spirit of God." 1 Corinthians 2:11 (TPT)

"For his Spirit joins with our spirit to affirm that we are God's children." Romans 8:16 (NLT)

We are spiritual beings in an earthly body and we are the only creatures God gave dominion of the earth to. In other words, we are the only creatures who have authority to govern the earth. This means we are in charge of the earth; we have the ability to rule it, direct it, and solve problems in it.

Myles Munroe, an evangelist and ordained minister, taught, "The only creature that has legal authority on earth is a human." He further says, "Any spirit outside of a body is illegal on planet earth. Therefore, for God to get anything done on earth He has to obey His own word." God always keeps His own Word. In His Word, the Bible we read,

"For You have magnified Your word above all Your name."
Psalm 138:2 (NKJV)

God's Word is so important to Him that He has set it above His own name. This means that God greatly honors His own Word and will not break it. If God were to break it He would be a liar, and how could any of us trust Him? The Truth is, He has never broken His Word and will not. Therefore, we can trust His Word when it shows us a spirit needs a body in order to function on earth. That is why God chooses people to work, to move, and change things.

Myles Munroe, one of my absolute favorite teachers, also said, "If anything is going to be done on earth legally, it has to be done by a spirit with a body." If we were to go to our Bibles to support this idea, where do we find God operating without a body? When God led the people out of slavery in Egypt He used Moses. With the Great Flood God used Noah. When God took out Goliath He used David. When God took out Jezebel he used Jehu. When God saved Nineveh He used Jonah. When God came down to earth to save the whole human race from their sins and an eternity spent in hell He came through Mary and in the bodily form of Jesus.

I became excited as I understood this. God uses humans to work here on earth. God uses us to do His work here. And God wants to use you and me to do mighty things on earth that will advance His Kingdom, to bring Heaven on earth. Jesus Himself prayed this:

"Your kingdom come Your will be done
On earth as it is in heaven."
Matthew 6:10 (NKJV)

God's original plan for us was to govern the earth as an extension of Heaven. Do you think there are any problems in Heaven? Sickness? Disease? Relationship problems? Paralyzed lives crying out for meaning? NO! Jesus prayed God's will be done here on earth as it is in Heaven. How will that Kingdom come? It will come through humans – you and me.

Want to see your relationships impacted for Christ? Your family, communities, cities set free from the vast array of problems? God wants us to impact those around us for His Kingdom here on earth. This is why repentance is necessary. We change the way we think to align with the truth of God's Word of who we are. As a result, others will be drawn to our Father and will want to change the way they think too.

How Is Repentance Powerful?

Repentance is powerful; it positions us to be used by God in greater ways than we have experienced in our past and in greater ways than we could imagine possible for our future. It prepares us for the ministry God designed for us in the beginning. If we want to be equipped and empowered to live out our calling for Yahweh's Kingdom then we must learn to make repentance a part of our lives.

Continuing with the house cleaning analogy, God gave me a visual of repentance to help change the way I think. Houses can be used to entertain guests, and when I entertain guests in my house I am in the habit of tidying things up. I do not want anyone thinking I am a slob or a poor house keeper. When people just pop in for a visit unannounced I am often horrified. Without fail the surprise guests seem to show up at the worst times – when my house is a disaster. Frantically throwing stuff into my bedroom and shutting the door, I'd then apologize repeatedly to my guests for the mess. If they had only called I wouldn't be so embarrassed. What a nightmare!

What would be a greater nightmare is the thought of important people, people of great influence, stopping in unannounced and seeing my mess. This is where the Lord took me. He had me imagine having a house where any kind of guests may come to my door at any time. What if a person of royalty or high government came knocking on my door wanting to come in and discuss how they would like me to help them impact the community. If they were to come today, what kind of condition would my house be in? How would I likely respond if my house looked like an episode of *Hoarders*? Honestly, I would be thoroughly embarrassed. I would be at my guests' mercy to reschedule the meeting to give myself time to clean up all the junk.

Repentance, God showed me, is like cleaning out all the junk from my house and committing to take continued action for keeping it clean. That way I would always be ready for whoever stops by, whether announced or unannounced. In this analogy the house represents me as the whole person. In reality I never know who I may run into – out in public, knocking on my door, on-line, Zoom gatherings, or phone calls – and I don't know if or how God wants to use me to impact a particular person or group of people. The practice of repentance is keeping myself prepared and positioned to be used by God. This cleaning house analogy also helped me to see more clearly who I am, what my purpose is and the great significance I have to Jesus.

My mother was used by the devil to blind me from the truth of who I am. She was used to help fill my "house" with junk and develop poor "house-keeping" habits, which were wrong patterns of thinking. Somewhere along the way these wrong patterns of thinking felt like a sick *normal*, and I hated it. I hated living in the cluttered, overwhelming, suffocating mess of my house, but I didn't know I needed to "clean" (repent), let alone how. I didn't know how to do self-maintenance, how to deal with unwanted, heavy thoughts and emotions in my heart and mind. Repentance holds the power to change and bring peace to my heart, mind and direction in life.

Repentance is necessary for a healed heart. I am important to God and He wants and needs me. My wounded heart has caused me to stop functioning the way I was designed to function. The good news is God has created a healing program, and repentance is a powerful part of this program. He desires to fully restore my heart because He loves me, He cares about me and He needs me to impact my world for His Kingdom. In Yahweh's Kingdom I am valued, I am worth it, I am desirable and I am powerful.

The Greater Effect Of Repentance

I have never had to look far to see problems in my family, community, city and world. There are problems everywhere. I believe God wants us healed so He can use us to be a solution to a problem, big or small. This shift in my perspective allowed me to see the greater effect of repentance. Repentance and ultimately my healed heart isn't just for me, it is for Him. Remember, God chooses to intervene into the earth's problems through humans. Therefore, we need to allow God to heal our hearts so He can use us to solve problems and bring His Kingdom here on earth.

With that said, it brings clarity as to why Satan has targeted children, vulnerable and weak, to prevent them from finding their true identity in Christ. More recently I even hesitated writing this book because I didn't feel like my story was significant enough to make an impact. It took years for me to understand that I don't need to have a horrific life story to be used by God and I didn't need horrific events to happen to be stopped by the devil. It may only take one word to create a small scar to keep any of us from fulfilling our destiny. Satan doesn't need to pull out all the weapons on every child. One hurtful word has the ability to deeply wound our hearts so badly our entire growth and purpose as a human is hindered.

This is why repentance is so powerful. Clean the house, get rid of the junk and change our thinking patterns to align with His Word so God can come in and use us to make a powerful impact for His Kingdom. I am motivated to make repentance a regular part of my life. Why? Because I am excited to see how God is going to empower me for the powerful ministry and secret missions He has for me in advancing His Kingdom and drawing others closer to Himself.

How Do I Repent?

Like I mentioned, I did not grow up in a home where repentance was taught and practiced. I think my first introduction to repentance was at youth group at a local Pentecostal church. During my time with YWAM I received more instruction on repentance, what it is, why it is essential as a believer and how to do it. Repentance is simple. It is not for the over-zealous Christian; it is not only to the advanced believers and you don't have to take classes on it to make sure you are doing it "right." Repentance is between us and God. It does not have to be done at a church, with a pastor or other religious leader. It can be done in the privacy of our own home and by ourselves.

My first real experience with repentance was when I was babysitting at 14 years old. After putting the children to bed I had this overwhelming sense of sorrow well up deep in my belly. I had been going in a direction with some friends, a direction I knew God didn't want me to go in. In the living room of my neighbor's house, with their children in bed, I fell on my knees. Sorrow flowed out of me in the form of tears. Sobbing quite violently for a while, the emotional release was exactly what I needed. I hadn't realized how weighty my disobedience had become. After repenting I felt so light, refreshed, and joy bubbled where the sorrow had been.

To repent, first acknowledge a need for help. I needed help; I didn't want to live like this anymore. I didn't want to feel yucky, heavy and angry anymore. I didn't want to act out of my yucky, heavy, angry feelings anymore. I didn't want the pain of my abuse to consume my thought life anymore. I couldn't change on my own; I needed help. I acknowledged out loud to God, that I needed help and it was His help I wanted.

Second, confess sins to God. Sin is choosing not to do the will of

God according to His Word and Spirit. Sometimes that "choosing" happens subconsciously without our knowing. For example, the lies and false ideas we came into agreement with about ourselves, God and the world around us. Confessing our sin can be admitting to the sins we know of and acknowledging the sins we have committed subconsciously as the Lord reveals them to us. Sin separates us from God. In our desire to just be closer to Him we can ask Him to show us any sins, false ideas or lies we have cooperated with.

After asking, sit quietly and patiently and allow the Lord to prompt. Most of the time it will just pop into your mind or pop out of your mouth; you have an inner knowing the Lord just revealed something to you. Other times in my life the Lord reveals sins through something I read, hear or through another person. As He reveals these sins to us confess them. This confession can be as easy as saying, "Father, I confess my sin of _____ to you, please forgive me."

Third, outwardly declare your refusal to continue in this sin. For example,

"Father, I refuse to continue _____ (name the sin) _____. I repent of this, and I am choosing to change the way I think, feel and act in regards to _____ (name the sin) _____ I want to change and never operate under this ever again. Please help me."

Fourth, ask God to send the sin, false idea or lie away. Imagine yourself nailing it to the cross where Jesus died for your sins. Or see yourself tying a weight on the sin and dropping it into the deepest part of the ocean. You could imagine it burning up, never to be seen again. Whatever the imagery is that helps you to visualize the sin going away forever, close your eyes and watch it in your mind. Sometimes I ask God to give me an image and He does. Then, say out loud, "Father, I ask You to send _____ (name the sin) _____ away from me forever."

Finally, ask God to give you something in place of what you just repented from. You just gave something up, maybe something pretty big, now it is time to fill the void this sin left with something good, something from God. For example, when I repented from cooperating with the lie that I am selfish God gave me confidence in exchange. In exchange for anger God gave me peace in my body, heart and mind. When I repented of my disappointment in Him God gave me joy. When I repented all the hate I had been hanging on to God exchanged that for compassion. Whatever the sin is you are repenting of ask God to give you something in exchange, and patiently wait for Him to speak to your spirit giving you your answer.

"Father, I give you _____ (name the sin) _____. What do You want to give me in its place?"

My Repentance

This chapter has detailed how I needed to repent from believing, identifying and cooperating with the lie that I am selfish. Even though this lie was engraved in me through my mother, God revealed it to me later in life. When I moved out of my mother's house and was no longer under her authority I should not have been operating in the same mindset as if I was. I should have chosen to put myself under the authority of God's Word, but I didn't. And in my defense I didn't know I needed to. I had the strong desire to get out from under my mother's influence, but I had not been trained or equipped to make the transition spiritually.

The junk that collected in my mind and heart (hurt, pain and scars from my mother) has taken years to shed, peeling off the layers I created around each wound and repenting for hanging on to it all. Without me knowing it my wounded heart became part of my identity, and yet it never should have been. My identity should be completely in Christ. Now I know and truly believe these are the scariest people to the devil and the most powerful people in the world: those who are completely confident in who they are in Christ, fully knowing who they are, their purpose and having nothing to hide.

Unboxed Prayer

Here was my prayer of repentance from selfishness:

Father, I confess that I have believed, identified with and have been operating under the lie that I am selfish. Even though I would tell myself that I wasn't, I had no idea that I actually identified with this lie to the point of it dictating daily decisions. I see how much it has affected my life, hindering me from being who I want to be and doing what I want to do. This lie owned me and I didn't even know it. Please forgive me, Father, for believing and cooperating with this lie. I repent of listening to selfishness as if it was who I was. I want to change the way I think, act and feel about myself. I refuse to believe this lie anymore. I ask You, Father, to send this lie that selfishness is my identity far away from me. I cannot send it on my own. I cannot change on my own. I nail it to the cross and watch it burn up with tiny pieces of black ash disappearing into the air. Father, instead of selfishness, what do You want to give me? I receive confidence.

In the mighty name of Yeshua, AMEN!

FOUR

Responsibility, My Dynamic Shift

One afternoon, I walked into the kitchen and noticed my brother-in-law struggling to cut a pineapple, a pineapple I had offered to cut at the lunch table just hours before with my whole family present. I said I would take care of cutting the pineapple when my mom made a comment about either not wanting to cut it or not knowing quite how to cut it. I can't remember which, I just remember saying I would do it since I had the experience. Having lived in southern China for two years I had cut quite a few pineapples using a technique I had witnessed many times from the multiple street vendors. Rather than let my brother-in-law struggle, I decided to offer my assistance. My sister, who had been standing nearby heard my offer and didn't allow my brother-in-law to answer, but chose to answer for him. Annoyed, she responded, "He is doing just fine. I don't know why you have to be so angry."

I walked away, as I have learned to do. I walked away irritated that my sister has followed in my mother's footsteps, calling me angry as if it were my identity, whether anger was present in me or not. I had offered assistance; I wasn't angry. These mean, thoughtless jabs I had become accustom to as the normal way my family speaks to me. When I have tried to defend myself it seemed to be taken as an invitation for verbal abuse, reminding me over and over again I am *a problem* that will never change.

This particular incident, however, my sister's response revealed something to me about my childhood that would become another piece of my healing journey.

My sister called me angry. She called me angry when I was not angry. Yet walking away from the kitchen I found myself feeling anger because I was being told how I felt rather than being free to express my feelings for myself. The funny thing is this was normal for me. My family, especially my mother, calling me angry, whether I was actually angry or not, and the accusation would create anger in me for not allowing me to express myself. My mother labeled me, spoke over me and treated me as a child with an anger problem. This is so incredibly abnormal. Reflecting on this kitchen incident I realized it was no longer just my mom who was verbally and emotionally abusing me. Her repeated behavior toward me taught my siblings that this is how we talk to and treat Kari. I found myself wondering *when did my siblings start speaking to me like this? When did they start calling me angry and speaking anger over me like my mother?* I have no answer.

This new revelation had my mind going a million miles a minute trying to figure it out. The way my mother spoke to me became such a normal way of life that my siblings picked it up somewhere along the way, also believing and acting on the lie. As long as I can remember my mother spoke anger over me. She called me angry even if I wasn't. She would create anger in me by accusing me of anger, and when I would defend my own feelings she would repeat herself with emphasis, "You are angry because you are *always* angry." When I tried to stand strong and assure her that I wasn't, her well-known line was, and I can still hear her voice saying it in my head, "You were born angry, you came out angry and you will always be angry." According to my mother I am an angry person and would never change.

That sentence, "You came out angry," wrecked my young innocent heart. These harsh words repeatedly spoken over me as a child stole my innocence, joy and pride. This treatment was learned by both my brother and sister. I was not allowed to experience love from my family because I was the angry one. And no one would ever allow me to forget it. The repeated voice of my mother saying, "You were born angry," or "You came out angry," were words that also communicated *you are not worthy of being loved, not worthy of being heard and not worthy of expressing yourself.*

With no one to defend my innocence I went deeper and deeper into myself, unable to even learn who I was. Anger was expressed because I wasn't allowed to express any other emotion. According to my mother I would always be angry. Even if I wanted to change she made me feel like anger was the incurable disease I would suffer from all the days of my life. Oh, how the devil is a liar.

On the occasion when I tried to verbally explain to my mother how her words and actions were hurtful and she responded, "I don't feel I've done anything wrong," it was a knife to the heart. I think that phrase was carved on my flesh that day, and I have allowed Satan to repeat it to me over and over and over again. That quote was probably the most hurtful thing I have ever heard my mother say. Here I am pouring out my heart, which was always so difficult for me, and it felt like she took advantage of my vulnerability to hurt me. This was when I realized I may never get an, "I'm sorry, do you forgive me?" It wasn't happening.

After crying out to God many times, wondering *what is wrong with me*, time and time again my loving God would ask me to trust Him and let Him be my loving parent. Time and time again I knew that was what I needed to do, that was what I wanted to do, but I always seemed to turn back and allow the pain my parents caused to control me. The anger and the pain would fester inside. Anger and pain started to feel comfortable. I knew it wasn't the real me. Sadly I was right where the devil wanted me. As long as I allowed the anger and pain to fester, I would not fulfill my purpose in the Kingdom of God and my heart wouldn't heal.

In my later teens and into my adult years I stopped verbally asking for forgiveness; the reactions from my mother were too painful. It seemed to hurt more each time, so I couldn't do it in person anymore. Instead I started writing letters. Even with the letters I received no favorable response. In fact I received no response at all.

As I mentioned, in my early adult years I started getting

counseling at church for the emotional abuse. Yet the lies that the abuse wasn't significant enough to matter made me feel guilty for not being able to deal with it myself and move on to a happy, healthy life. All the abuse came to a head when my husband witnessed how my parents were treating me

My husband wanted me to move out of their home at that time but I thought I needed to *be an adult* and tough it out. But after breaking down at work from the emotional abuse and being counseled by my boss, a highly respected, Holy Spirit-filled Christian elder, I wrote my final letter and moved out. I asked for forgiveness for anything I could think of and told my mother I wanted to have a healthy relationship with her but without a change in behavior in each of us it would never happen.

I had to set up a boundary or else the story would always be the same. I proposed that we sit down and talk with a mediator, any respectable Christian leader of my mother's choice about our current relationship and come to an agreement about changed behaviors. Otherwise, I could not return. Just forgiving them wasn't enough. If my mother didn't repent and turn from her abusive behavior I would always get hurt.

And that was that. I left the note on my bed when I moved out. Later, when I returned to my parents' house to get something I forgot, I saw the letter open so I know it was received. Even so, she never brought up the note. She never asked why I moved out. She didn't call. NOTHING!

I love my mom, but I had to make the heartbreaking decision to separate myself from her, from the abuse, to be able to work on my healing. It was time to stop seeking my healing from her and take personal responsibility for my own healing. For the sake of my kids I did keep in contact with my mother; I wanted them to know their grandmother.

Taking Personal Responsibility

Taking personal responsibility for my choices is not always easy. The more I practice it, it gets easier, but there are times when it is very difficult. When I truly understood in my heart that my choices determine my future and I could not blame anyone else I began to see positive change in my life.

One perspective which helped me understand the depth of personal responsibility was when I realized I'll stand before the throne of God someday. When I do I won't be giving an account for the life of someone else. I will be giving an account for my life and only my life. According to the Word of God I am responsible before the Lord for myself and will, on that Day of Judgement, give an account to Him (Romans 14). With this in mind I need to choose to do what is right even if no one else is.

Taking personal responsibility means I believe I have the ability to choose and control my own actions. I choose to take the credit or blame for my own actions, whatever the outcome is. I own the fact that I have the ability to make choices for my life; no one, not even my mother, has the power to make choices for me unless I give her that power. As an adult learning to own every choice I make, thought, word or action has helped me grow as a person and adapt in a healthy way to events and situations in life that are out of my control.

The Dynamic Shift

Learning to take personal responsibility dynamically shifted my thinking which in turn transformed my life. It took me from feeling hopeless to being hopeful, existing to living, angry to compassionate, sad to joyful. It took me from being abused to being used to advance the Kingdom of God. In John 5 we read about a time when Jesus addressed a lame man who was waiting to be healed. Here we can clearly see the powerful impact of the outcome for choosing to take personal responsibility.

"After this there was a feast of the Jews, and Jesus went up to Jerusalem. Now there is in Jerusalem by the Sheep *Gate* a pool, which is called in Hebrew, Bethesda, having five porches. In these lay a great multitude of sick people, blind, lame, paralyzed, waiting for the moving of the water. For an angel went down at a certain time into the pool and stirred up the water; then whoever stepped in first, after the stirring of the water, was made well of whatever disease he had. Now a certain man was there who had an infirmity thirty-eight years. When Jesus saw him lying there, and knew that he already had been *in that condition* a long time, He said to him, 'Do you want to be made well?'" John 5: 1-6 (NKJV)

Allow me to draw attention to some specifics in this passage. Jesus asked the lame man, "Do you really want to get well?" Notice, Jesus already knew the lame man had been in that condition for a long time and you would think the obvious answer to this question would be, "Yes, I want to get well," especially since the lame man had positioned himself at this healing pool. This begs the question, "How, in 38 years, has he not made it to the pool yet?" There are clearly layers to this man's story not seen by the outside world that are not obvious. Just like us what is seen by the world on our outside does not portray the many layers of our story leading to our current situation.

This verse in Proverbs stuck out to me this morning:

"Don't expect anyone else to fully understand
both the bitterness and the joys
of all you experience in your life."
Proverbs 14:10 (TPT)

Every person can fit into this scripture. The lame man, myself and you, we all have life experiences no one can fully understand. There is only one person who truly knows us and can pierce right to the heart of any issue. That person is Jesus. *Do you really want to get well?* Just like Jesus asked the lame man, I asked myself *do I really want to get well?* Do you really want your heart healed? Do you want to be free from the bondages of your emotionally abusive mother? Do you want to live a life of radical freedom and joy? Do you want to have the life you were created for? I seriously asked myself these questions because some women don't want to get well. Yes, let's be honest…it's true.

Some women, and we all know some, but please do not list names, are comfortable in their miserable lives. They love to complain, grumble, criticize, gossip and are always making excuses for this, that and the other thing. These women love the attention they get as they share their never-ending sob stories, inviting others to have sympathy on them. These women feel sorry for themselves and they love the attention they receive from having others feel sorry for them too. Hear this: these women are not healed. They have no idea who they truly are nor what powerful purpose God created them for. These women have lowered themselves to self-sabotage and turned a dull ear to truth. They are not walking out the Kingdom of Yahweh. I don't want to be one of these women.

Do you really want to get well? My answer is *YES* and I really wanted this healing. No matter the cost I chose to set it in my heart and mind I would get it. I was determined to be healed from my heart wounds. Even though I had been trained to self-sabotage I had a choice to listen to and apply truth, especially when it was uncomfortable and drew a kind of attention from others I had never experienced before. I was and still am determined to be a woman of truth. Speak truth over yourself even if it feels like no one else is. Every time my mother said, "You came out angry," or "You are just an angry person and will always be angry," she was speaking a lie over me. I replace that lie with truth. I am not an angry person. I will not own that lie. I am loving.

I am just now reminded of a recent story I need to share. It shows how good our God is at reminding us of the truth of who we are. I recently attended a Voice of the Apostles conference in Virginia, and while at that conference a man I have never met felt led to pray for me. In a crowd of hundreds of people this random man began to pray for me. The prayer quickly went to speaking words over me and giving words he believed God was telling him to tell me. One thing he said was God wanted me to know love would ooze from me. I would leave footprints of love wherever I go. This word was incredibly significant to me since the majority of my life anger was spoken over me. But God, my Creator, was speaking truth over me. I was not created to be angry, but I was created to leave footprints of love. I choose to align myself with God's truth; I am a lover.

Continuing with the account of the lame man, we read:

"The sick man answered Him, 'Sir, I have no man to put me into the pool when the water is stirred up; but while I am coming, another steps down before me.'
Jesus said to him, 'Rise, take up your bed and walk.' And immediately the man was made well, took up his bed, and walked."
John 5:7-9 (NKJV)

The lame man in John 5 couldn't walk, but I like to imagine that everything else worked from the waist up – his arms, his hands, his fingers, his eyes, his brain. You would think that if a person was determined to be healed they would have figured out a way to make it to the pool in 38 years. Even if he dragged himself using his own hands he very well could have made it there at some point in 38 years. What we do read is the lame man was sitting and waiting for someone else. Could you imagine, what if the lame man was truly determined? I like to think he could have laid down on the edge of the pool, leaning over the edge, so the slightest force would cause him to fall into the healing waters. He would sit like he was waiting for the moment the waters were stirred by the angel. That would be a picture of true determination.

The man Jesus approached was not determined and had not taken personal responsibility for his own healing. He lacked hope. He had aligned himself with defeat and accepted this miserable way of life. We cannot be like him. We cannot sit around waiting for someone else to be responsible for our healing. For many years I remained bitter because I believed my healing would come from my mother. I wanted her to heal me. I longed for the day she would hear me and see me for who God created me to be. My heart was desperate to be loved by her, a love I never had yet innately believed existed. *If only my mother would see how greatly she has damaged me through every criticizing word, every twisted and manipulating plot, every moment of belittling, every time she ignored or rejected me.* I truly thought, *if she repented of the way she treated me and asked for forgiveness, I would be instantly healed, because, of course, I would instantly forgive her.* Yet, this has never happened. And honestly I believe it hasn't happened because if it had, I never would have learned how true healing comes from God.

By relying on my mother's repentance for my healing I had given her power over my life once again; power she never should have had and actually it didn't belong to her. If my healed heart came the way I wanted it come I would never have discovered and understood my own power of personal responsibility or experienced the dynamic shift by bringing life back to a hopeless body. I also never would have experienced a deepened level of surrendering to my Savior or discover the purpose for which He created me. I sat around too long, waiting for someone else to heal me when they couldn't. I needed to take personal responsibility for my own healing. So I got up and went to the pool of living waters, the presence of our God, Yahweh.

Before we move on from this account of Jesus and the lame man, I really feel the need to explore another possible excuse in the lame man's reasoning for not having made it to the pool. This is an excuse I relate to. Yes, the lame man was waiting for someone else to put him into the healing waters of the pool rather than positioning himself due to his lack of determination, but maybe he was comfortable in his misery? What if the lame man didn't make it to the pool because he felt it was just too hard? Yes, this excuse very well could have been *it was flat out too hard.*

That got my attention. How many times in my life have I avoided doing something because the task felt too hard? Or how many times in my life did I feel it would be easier if someone else did my task for me? How often have I sat around hoping someone else will do the dishes, right? A picture that just came to mind was one of a young child refusing to put on their own shoes. They would rather whine on the floor that it is "too hard" waiting for an adult to put the shoes on for them. I could seriously go on and on with examples here, but the point is I could waste a lot of valuable time waiting for someone else to do something for me that I can do myself.

Taking personal responsibility for my own healed heart was not easy. Too many people have never seen their breakthrough because the journey became *too hard.* No one said it was going to be easy, and I am here sharing from personal experience it is not. When something gets hard we have two options: give up and never experience the breakthrough of healing and true joy, or press in harder even though it hurts.

"Dear children, you belong to God. You have not accepted the teachings of the false prophets. That's because the one who is in you is powerful. He is more powerful than the one who is in the world."
1 John 4:4 (NIRV)

When the emotional struggle gets tough I remember He who is in me, the Spirit of the living God, He is stronger than anything or anyone in this world. I have the power of the Holy Spirit living inside of me to help me do the hard stuff. I was never created to do the hard parts of life on my own even though I feel I was conditioned to. If everything was easy I wouldn't need God. How sad would that be?

After Jesus asked the lame man if he wanted to be well the lame man responded with an excuse. Jesus did not entertain the lame man's excuse for one moment. Jesus gave a bold invitation for healing. The lame man had a choice either to remain where he was, hoping and longing, or to accept the invitation and do what Jesus said. The lame man literally had a word from the Lord he could take action on that word or not. That was all he needed – to take action on the word the Lord Jesus gave him.

All we need is to take action on the Word of God. It is our responsibility to know the Word of God, apply the Word and to seek intimacy with the Word. When I hit a wall in my healing journey where I felt stuck or when the journey became too difficult I did not give up. I remember I am in a war with the devil who hates me. He targeted me as a child to prevent me from being who I am created to be. He will not allow this journey to be easy. The devil will meet me in the quiet places to get me to entertain the painful memories of the past. He will try to clothe me in depression and loneliness again, weighing me down making me feel helpless, worthless and hopeless. The devil wants me discouraged.

Please remember, feelings may be real but they are not always the truth. Do not allow feelings to lead this healing journey – it must be led by the Word of God.

Preparation In The Wilderness

Taking personal responsibility does not mean life is instantly easy. Sometimes owning our choices, including the mistakes, can lead to a time in our own form of a wilderness. Even though our wilderness can be uncomfortable, difficult and exhausting, if we continue to make the choice to fight for our healing and follow the Word of God our wilderness time will strengthen our character, develop successful habits, gain respect from others, teach how make better choices, and also help us become dependable and hard working. Ultimately our wilderness time will be a training ground for conquering greater obstacles in the future which can lead to greater successes and a greater me, you, us. It's like a refiner's fire gets the impurities out, freeing us to be who God created us to be.

I want us to explore a couple more places in Scripture to really see the significance of taking personal responsibility in our lives and taking action on the Word of the Lord.

"When Pharaoh let the people go, God did not lead them on the road through the Philistine country, though that was shorter. For God said, 'If they face war, they might change their minds and return to Egypt.'" Exodus 13:17 (NIV)

Here we see God chose to lead the Israelites not on the easy path. When the Israelites came out of Egypt God wanted to take them to the Promised Land, however it was currently occupied by other people. Yes, the Israelites had a word from the Lord that the land was theirs, yet just as we saw with the lame man, the word alone is not what brings about the promise. It is when His people take action on the word. The Israelites weren't going to have the promise handed to them on a silver platter; they would have to war for it. Being fresh out of slavery, the Lord knew they weren't ready to war for their Promised Land. For this reason God took His people on the path that would prepare them for the war that was ahead.

For years I questioned God about why my healing wasn't instantaneous. Why did I continue to suffer mild anxiety attacks every time my mom's name displayed on my phone? Why did I still become completely exhausted being in her presence from using my inner strength to hold my defenses strong? I never realized the healing of a wounded heart could take so much time. Even though I do believe some healings are instantaneous, the truth is, a lot of healings take time. Understanding this truth helps to eliminate frustration. We are called to be free and to fulfill a powerful purpose. In those frustrating moments let's not give up or give in to the lie that healing is too hard, it is taking too long or maybe it isn't for us. That is a lie straight from hell.

We are called by Him. Read this and believe it. In the moments of darkness may we never doubt what God has told us in the light. We are called out of the land of slavery, the bondages of emotional abuse, and are on our journey to our promised land, a place of peace, joy and freedom where we get to be fully who we were made to be.

When our healing journey feels long and exhausting let's remind ourselves of the Israelites. Remember, they were called to the Promised Land and took the long way to get there. The Israelites were in preparation for many years. Our healing may also take many years, but it doesn't have to be as long as the Israelites'. Their journey was extended as a consequence to their disobedience. During a moment of darkness they chose to doubt God's Word.

We can learn from their mistake and not allow our healing to take longer than it needs to. This may be our time in the wilderness, our time of preparation for what God will have us do in the future. How long we stay here in the wilderness is up to us. Stay focused and obedient to the Lord. It may feel tough right now, but keep moving forward. God has already told us the end of our story. If we choose to keep moving and stay obedient to Him we will come out of the wilderness prepared to fight whatever lies in the way of our full healing and fulfillment of our calling.

Faith In The Storm

One more example I love and want to share is from Mark 4:35-41. Jesus and His disciples set out in a boat to cross a lake. On their journey across the lake a hurricane-sized storm arose. The disciples experienced an array of emotions during this time of great trial: fear, worry, anxiety, terror, helplessness. We have all been there. Unexpected circumstances arise in life and we don't know what to do, so we tend to panic, stress out and fear the worst.

I don't know who said this, but I read it once somewhere: "The way God can show us He's in control is to put us in situations we can't control." The disciples could not control the weather just as we could not control the family we were born into nor the actions of our mothers (or anyone for that matter). We often cannot control the circumstances we find ourselves in, however we can control how we respond.

Despite the hurricane-sized storm the disciples found themselves in we read in Mark chapter 5 that they safely made it to the other side of the lake. Remember, it was Jesus who led the disciples to cross the lake at that time. Jesus was with them in the boat. He wasn't caught off guard or surprised by the storm. Calmly, Jesus reminded the disciples to have faith. Their faith that day revealed some of the power of the Kingdom of Yahweh.

When we follow Jesus we are not promised an easy stress-free life with smooth sailing. No, but we are promised that Jesus will be with us, and we are called to trust Him.

"And surely I am with you always, to the very end of the age."
Matthew 28:20 (NIV)

Jesus is with each of us through every storm we find ourselves in. Trust in Him and we will make it through to the other side, just as the disciples made it to the other side of the lake and the Israelites received their Promised Land.

How To Take Personal Responsibility

Taking personal responsibility is something we learn and practice. Every morning when we wake-up we get to decide what we think, say and do. I am in the practice of talking to my Heavenly Father as soon as I wake-up. "Thank you, Daddy, that I am Your favorite." Yes, I definitely say that sometimes. From there I start speaking truth over myself. "I am fabulous," "I am beautiful," "I am going to have an awesome day because I am in control of my attitude, my happiness, my love," and so on. For real though, we all need some reminders and encouragement on taking personal responsibility.

Here is a helpful list:

1) Know who you are and remind yourself frequently throughout the day. For example, I am a princess because my Daddy is the King of Kings, I am loved, I am a masterpiece, I am strong, I am valued, I am a good person, and I am a woman of my word.

2) Know you have control over your own thoughts, words and actions. Practice rebuking and correcting every thought, word or action that does not line up with the Word of God.

3) Stop blaming your mother (or anyone) for all your misfortunes. Blaming others will keep you in a victim mindset which prevents you from fully healing and personal growth.

4) Stop complaining. Ask yourself, how is the cup half full right now? Or just start praising Jesus. It is amazing how praising the Lord can calm your mind and spirit when all you want to do is grumble and complain (literally typing this for myself right now).

5) Choose not to take anything personal. In all honesty, is it really about you? Okay, typing to myself again. Jesus did say that we will be hated because of Him. Also, when people are being rude and disrespectful there is probably a reason that has nothing to do with us. They could also be going through abuse at home and just don't know how to deal with it.

6) Be present in the moment. Enjoy it. Ask God where He is in the moment and what He wants to say to you. Sometimes we are so caught up with the past or future we don't know how to enjoy the moments and be present with God in the now.

7) Ask yourself, what, right now, makes me happy? Try it. It can be fun. It may have you start laughing at the most inappropriate time, but I am totally okay with being happy even if no one else around me is.

8) Take action/be intentional. For example, sit still for a minute. Literally set a timer and envision the day while you are still in bed. What will you wear, eat, where will you drive to, who do you want to talk to? Then, get out of bed and go do it. I like to make daily to-do lists. I will even include things like prayer, ask God who I can bless today, text _____, worship break, take a

walk, and so on. Envisioning what you are going to do helps us be intentional with our time, especially spending time with the Lord. Being intentional about being in His presence could shift everything.

9) Admit your mistakes and learn from them. Everyone makes mistakes so do not beat yourself up over them. Allow yourself to celebrate a learning opportunity and the opportunity for personal growth.

10) Forgive yourself. No one except Jesus is perfect.

11) Be a person of your word. If you say you are going to do something, do it. On the flip side of that, do not say you can do something if you already know you can't due to time or resources.

12) Do not make excuses. Own your words and actions. Apologize if necessary.

13) Look for the good in people.

14) Breathe. Be still and take a moment. Breathe.

Unboxed Prayer

Dear Father,

Here I am, take all of me. I give You my wounds, I give You my mistakes, I give You my imperfect actions. I do not want to be paralyzed or dragged down with exhaustion trying to be who I am not designed to be. Give me the courage to own my actions and not make excuses. Deepen my understanding that I am not defined by my mistakes; I am defined by who You say I am. Today I shake off the mentality that guarding my wounded heart is an acceptable excuse for hurting others. I do not want to walk into my calling with the potential of hurting others. Today I shake off the shame. I shake off the guilt. I shake off the excuses. Today I step into my healing and my wholeness. Today, I declare I am Yours. Use me!

In the mighty name of Yeshua, AMEN!

FIVE

Surrender, My Gift

"Mom, what are you doing? You can come and sit at the front," I insisted as my mom took a seat in the back row by the door of the church I was getting married in. Trying to get my mother to be involved in the planning of my wedding felt like pulling teeth. She expressed next to no emotion. She wasn't excited to help me plan, prepare or even offer advice. I felt very alone in the wedding preparation process and had no idea what I was doing. God seemed to know my mother would be absent even though I held on to the hope she would step into the "mother-of-the-bride" role. Nope.

By divine appointment I was introduced to a newcomer at church, a beautiful woman who happened to be from Mexico. The pastor's wife had shared with her that I was engaged and my dream wedding would be on a beach. After meeting me she went right to talking about my wedding. It turned out that she loved planning weddings and it would be an honor for her if I allowed her to help plan a Mexican beach wedding. WOW! My dream wedding would really happen...God is so good. It was seriously a dream come true.

We soon started meeting together and this beautiful Mexican angel would share all her wedding recommendations and ideas. She was from a small town in Mexico on the coast and had many connections with family members and friends. She asked if I would be fine with the wedding being in her home town – preparations would be easier and we could possibly do more for less cost. After seeing some pictures I was absolutely in love with the idea of my wedding being in her home town.

Soon every meeting with my Mexican wedding angel was her

presenting wedding planning options and me making a choice. It was such an amazing experience. My wedding angel found a gorgeous resort on the beach, and with the information she gave me I made the reservations. Then, there were the meal choices – I chose the chicken and beef. We made arrangements for the wedding and reception to be outside on the beach. We also reserved a room for our "memories" video to be shown with a projector and screen. A reservation was made with Wedding Angel's best friend to do my hair. She gave us the flower shop information so I could pick out my flowers, I chose red roses. Wedding Angel's family owned a restaurant where we had the rehearsal dinner. Almost every detail was taken care of. My Mexican Wedding Angel was so easy and kind to work with. I truly felt all I really needed to do was find a dress and show up. My Heavenly Father truly looked after me and every detail.

In the height of the wedding planning my mother offered to go dress shopping with me. I was really surprised, considering I had felt she lacked involvement and interest in my life, but I was excited to take the offer. I was looking forward to bonding with her and seeing her step into this "mother-of-the-bride" role. Even though we had a rough past I truly thought she would step up and be there for me. This was a wedding after all, a union, a celebration…it was a big deal. Her first born was beginning a new chapter, making the choice of committing to a forever partner in this adventure we call life. I desired for my mother to see me follow the path my Heavenly Father has set before me, to expand His ministry through me by my union with a God-fearing man. This was legitimately one of the most significant events of my life, and I wanted my mother to see it as such.

The dress shopping, over all, was enjoyable, I have no real complaints. It took a lot longer and far more travel than I originally had imagined. Who knew there were so many ugly wedding dresses out there! Dress shopping is definitely not on my favorite things to do list. I sifted, waded and fought through thousands of ugly dresses and scouted every inch of Vancouver from North Vancouver to downtown to New Westminster and everywhere in between to find *the one.* Maybe I am just super picky, but really I am just a girl who knew exactly what she wanted and I wasn't going to settle for less.

My mother was really good throughout the whole scavenger hunt. I explained exactly what kind of dress I wanted: a simple white or ivory dress that was made with a light material. I was getting married in Mexico for crying out loud. I wanted a spaghetti strap, backless dress, with no lace and minimal to no beading. I really didn't think I was asking for too much – simple and pretty. My mother really heard what I wanted in a wedding dress and even kept me accountable when she saw me starting to compromise my vision in my frustration of not finding it. I was thankful she was there to keep me focused, especially when the sales women skilled in smooth and manipulative words were doing what they could to make a sale. Actually, only one sales woman was like that. My mother was encouraging when I was treated rudely by sales women who told me I wouldn't find what I was looking for. I think they were just frustrated they couldn't get a sale from me.

I remember we had a great lunch break at an Asian restaurant in North Vancouver and we both thought our waitress was invisible. Our waters would be filled, our dirty plates would disappear and we never remembered the waitress coming to take them. It was the strangest feeling. That waitress had some amazing skills in not disrupting the customers. Maybe she was some kind of waitress ninja.

Anyway, the good news is we found my dress, exactly what I wanted. To celebrate, my mom and I went out for steak. We deserved it. We had some really great food, good conversation and for a short time I felt loved and seen by her. She really stepped up for the wedding dress shopping, and I am very grateful for this beautiful memory I will hang on to.

I had such a great enjoyable experience with the wedding dress shopping my expectations for my mother's loving support for the rest of the wedding planning had risen quite high. Either intentional or not the rest of the wedding planning was less than pleasurable, and I don't know why. She told me she would take care of the wedding announcements and reception invitations. Having such a great wedding dress experience with her, I decided to trust her with these. I went to the shop, picked out the invitations and wrote out what I wanted written on them. I remember giving her a date for when I wanted those invitations because I wanted to mail them out by a certain date. I left to return to my job which was in another city. The times when I would check in she assured me she was taking care of it, so I chose not to worry.

When the date I was expecting those announcements and invitations to arrive I called my mom to see if they were in. I will never forget her reply, "I haven't ordered them yet." I was so clear in what I wanted and she had assured me, more than once, she was taking care of it. What was most frustrating is that she had no other wedding planning responsibilities because of my beautiful Mexican Wedding Angel. *I trusted you with this ONE thing...*

I lost it. I was beyond angry. Mostly I was angry with myself for thinking she had changed and I could trust her. Caught up in my emotions I began yelling at her on the phone. I was not okay and I was not about to act like I was. Later, God convicted me and I did call her back to apologize.

For the rest of the wedding planning and the wedding itself she acted like she didn't care and nothing was a big deal for her. My husband and I decided to have a small ceremony at our church in Alberta the day before going to Mexico. It was easier to have the Justice of the Peace perform a small ceremony in Canada than to deal with the international marriage paperwork. Our wedding was still in Mexico, but we took care of the legal side in Canada before we left.

I invited my mother to come to this Justice of the Peace ceremony honestly thinking she would want to be there. After all, I was her first child to get married. In truth, I wanted her to be there and I wanted her to *want* to be there. She did not give me the satisfaction. When we arrived at the church my mother took a seat at the very back of the sanctuary. "Mom, what are you doing? You can come and sit at the front," I insisted. She refused. Our friends who had come to witness our marriage asked if my mother was coming to the front. I told her she wants to be in the back. Surprised, my friend replied, "If it was my daughter getting married I would want to be in the front row." I didn't know what to say, but replied, "That's my mom."

The Justice of the Peace asked if my mother would join us at the front...my mother declined. All of us were shocked in the room. I had no explanation and my mother never gave one. At the wedding in Mexico guests would ask if this behavior was normal of my mother and I would reply, "Yes." She showed no emotion. There was a lack of involvement, interest, love, care, motherly affection, and joy. It was heartbreaking, but I didn't allow her behavior to ruin my day.

I had the best wedding ever. I was marrying the man of my dreams, in the location of my dreams and nothing was going to spoil my happiness and joy. The day was incredibly joyous. I have nothing to complain about because my Heavenly Father blessed me with the fairytale wedding I had longed for in my childlike heart.

In the end, I have beautiful memories of wedding dress shopping with my mother, and no one can take that away from me. I am choosing to not take her behavior personally because I believe it really isn't about me. There is something deeper there between my mother and God, and I refuse to allow her unhealed heart to derail me from enjoying special times or being all I am created to be. I choose to be intentional about looking at the good, surrendering my will to align with God's will and praising my Heavenly Father for His continuous blessings. I will also be intentional about being in His presence, knowing it changes everything – my mindsets, attitudes, pain, direction, outcomes, and my effect on the lives of others. The *surrendering* of my will to align with God's will is truly a gift for myself, setting me free from trying to control and change what I never can. Because guess what? I was not designed to control everything.

Finally, in this memory when I asked Jesus, "Where were You?" He revealed Himself to me sitting on the front row, a huge smile on

His face, looking more excited than I felt. He was a proud Father, soaking in the joy of His son and His daughter following His guidance, about to expand their impact for the Kingdom through their union, knowing they were made to advance together.

Looking at the face of Jesus in the front row of this memory, His smile had depth and mystery laced into it. I could tell He knew something about my husband and I; something so incredibly good, exciting, beautiful and rich. It looked as if He was about to explode from holding in this secret. I can't help but be curious as to what He was thinking. What did He know that we didn't? Well, everything! Who we would be, what we would do, the impact we would make, the family we would become…only He knows the grand scale and beauty of it all.

Surrender, What Does That Mean?

Often times I understand the meaning of most words and phrases, but when it comes to putting my understanding into words I find myself at a loss. I begin to question whether or not I truly understand the words for myself. The word *surrender* is one of those words. I understood it in the context of one army giving up the fight and saying they no longer want to fight the battle. That army would rather give their enemy or opponent the win than keep fighting. This often occurs when the surrendering side recognizes or acknowledges their opponent is too strong for them and there is no way of a win in their favor.

In this context, surrendering, in my understanding, has a negative connotation. Surrendering is associated with being weak, less than, losing and not being enough. It certainly isn't something anybody wants or seeks to do and it would not be considered a valuable gift to oneself. So what does it mean to *surrender* to God then? Or deeper still, to *surrender* my *will* to align with God's *will*?

I have never seen God as my enemy, yet now as I meditate on the word *surrender* I wonder if I have treated Him like one and didn't even know it. Maybe the struggle within myself was really a struggle between my *will* for my life, God's *will* for my life and Satan's *will* for my life.

To begin my word research I needed to define the terms *surrender* and *will*. The definition of *surrender* from dictionary.com includes, "to give oneself up, as into the power of another; submit or yield." *Will*, used as a noun, is defined, also by dictionary.com, as 1) "the faculty of conscious and especially of deliberate action," and, 2) "the power of control the mind has over its own actions: *the freedom of the will; power of choosing one's own actions: to have a strong or a weak will.*"

What stood out to me in both of these definitions was the word *power*. In the word *surrender* a person is recognizing the power of another. In the definition of the word *will* it highlights the power I hold – the power to control my mind, my actions, my words. I am immediately reminded of one of Myles Munroe's teachings when he taught that the *will* is the most powerful thing on this earth; even God Himself doesn't control it. This statement holds mind-blowing truth.

In Genesis we read how God created human beings with the ability to choose. We were given a great power at creation. God wasn't going to *make* us do what He designed us to do; He wanted us to choose it.

As I reflected on the truth of my *will*, my power, I recognized how I was deceived into thinking I am less powerful than I actually am. Lies were implanted in me at a very young age; I believed those lies, and then formed a belief about who I am and what I am capable of doing based on those lies. I gave examples of this in earlier chapters, but let me revisit the impact of those lies for a moment; the lies that caused me to perform less than who I am made to be. I have the power to choose, but if I keep choosing a certain way that diminishes my true capabilities, I'll continue to be stuck in a mundane life, wishing for more, yet feeling I'm not deserving of more.

I want the full, abundant life. I want to feel accomplished and whole, yet the one who planted the lie in me holds power in my life. When I partnered with the lie by believing it I gave him power.

Knowing this, I can choose to take the power back. I can choose to think different thoughts. I can choose to uplift myself with my own words. I can choose who I listen to and who I ignore. I can choose how I use my time. I can choose who influences me. I can choose to *surrender*.

Surrendering my will to God, as I understand, is recognizing His power is greater than mine and allowing Him not to control me but to teach, guide and counsel me to be all I am designed to be. After all, God is my Creator. He made me. He knows every part of my being – from every thought, to everything that makes my heart beat a little faster, to every little thing that makes me smile, to what I need to feel loved and whole. He knows me. I could waste a lot of time trying to figure out who I am on my own, which isn't always all bad, but there is an easier, faster way. Also there is so much value in *surrendering* my *will* to my Creator and allowing Him to gently guide me to be the best version of myself.

What Is The Value Of Surrendering?

Have you ever felt like you are behind in this journey called life? Do you ever wonder why it seems like others are more successful at life than you are? Have you ever felt like you can't break free from these invisible bondages formed from the impact of your emotionally abusive mother? I know I have. I have felt completely haunted by my mother heart wounds and wondered if I would ever be free from the chains that accompanied them. But I have exciting news: there is freedom! In fact, I had a revelation from the Lord that it wasn't actually my mother who was keeping me in bondage as I had believed for years…it was myself. I was keeping myself in bondage by trying to fix it on my own. I wasn't designed to fix my problems and heal my wounds by myself. I was designed to be in relationship with my Creator and allow Him to guide me, instruct me, talk to me, listen to me, and show me the way through every problem and every hurt.

90

I have come to love Proverbs 25:2. It has been such a great aid in helping me understand how I was designed. Below are two versions of the verse, however I encourage you to look this verse up in more translations and allow the Holy Spirit to use each one to guide you into a deeper understanding of who you are designed to be.

"It is God's privilege to conceal things and the king's privilege to discover them." Proverbs 25:2 (NLT)

"God conceals the revelation of his word in the hiding place of his glory. But the honor of kings is revealed by how they thoroughly search out the deeper meaning of all that God says." Proverbs 25:2 (TPT)

From this verse, I first want to talk about the word *kings* with the lowercase *k*. In order to do that I want us to be clear on who is the *King* with the uppercase *K*. In Scripture Jesus is referred to as the King of Kings in multiple places (1 Timothy 6:15, Revelation 1:5, 17:14). Jesus is the King of Kings, Jesus is the Son of God, Jesus is the Word of God (John 1:1-3). Jesus was with God and was God in the beginning at creation. Therefore, the King of Kings, the *King* with the uppercase K, is not only Jesus, but our Creator. The one who designed us is the one who sits on the heavenly throne and rules over the heavenly Kingdom, the same Kingdom Jesus taught us to request its manifestation on earth through the Lord's Prayer (Matthew 6).

Our Creator and our King designed us in His image (Genesis 1:27), He is the King with the uppercase *K* and we are His image, the kings with the lowercase *k*, designed to rule and to reign and to have dominion over specific areas that are unique to us as individuals. Our purpose is unique because what we are called to have dominion over in our life is unique. We are the lowercase *kings*.

For the sake of making this a little more personal, we are *queens*. Read the Proverbs 25 verse again, and instead of reading *kings* put in your name in as *queen* _____. Let that sink into your soul a little bit.

Second, I want to address our *honor* and *privilege* as queens. In Proverbs 25:2 our God, who is our Creator, has purposefully hid His revelations of His Word in His glory, and it is our *honor* and *privilege* to find them. Our Creator has hidden His revelations because He wants us to search for them and find them. In this verse the Lord revealed to me that I am designed to search for revelations inside His Word. This answers the question, "Why hasn't God just downloaded to me my full purpose and the entire road map for my life?" He hasn't downloaded everything about us to us because we were designed to search for them and find them in Him. He didn't hide these things because He is a big fat meanie; He hid them because He designed us to be in relationship with Him, spending time with Him to find the treasure of who we were made to be.

It is an *honor* and *privilege* to "thoroughly search out the deeper meaning of all that God says" because that means we are spending time with the King, the most supreme, sovereign ruler EVER! No meeting with our King and Creator should ever be the same. Each time is an opportunity for fresh revelation of who we are as queens, what area we were designed to reign in and how we were designed to reign our God-given territory. Every meeting is an opportunity for fresh revelation of who our God and King is and who we are in and with Him. We were never designed to figure out who we are and how we fit into this messed up world by ourselves. We were designed to rule and reign a unique, God-given territory, in relationship with and under the rule and reign of the Almighty King of Kings. As I write this, I am feeling so empowered, and I pray you are as well. We were not only created to be free, but to rule and reign in power.

The value of *surrendering* our *will* to align with God's *will* is discovering our unique and powerful purpose. As we *surrender* our *will* to spend time with our Creator we learn how to exercise the authority we have been given with our purpose, and He equips us to completely fulfill our role as queens in our specific areas. *Surrendering* may be the most powerful gift to ourselves to operate as the queens we were made to be.

Jehu's Surrendering Example

Surrendering our *will* to align with the *will* of God reminds me of one of my all-time favorite Bible stories, 2 Kings 9, when Jehu receives a word from the Lord and rides into Jezreel to take out evil Queen Jezebel. Here we read that Elisha instructed a man from amongst the prophets to go to Jehu (an army officer) and take him to a quiet place away from his friends, pour a flask of oil on his head and anoint him King over Israel. This messenger did exactly as he was instructed.

After receiving this word from the messenger Jehu could have compiled a list of excuses, much like we listed for the lame man in John 5, preventing him from fulfilling this unique and powerful purpose. He could have easily ignored the word altogether, concluding the messenger was a crazy man who was completely out of his mind. Or he could have believed the messenger, but then chose to do nothing with it after remembering the strength and wickedness of the current leaders: Joram the king of Israel, his mother Jezebel and Ahaziah the king of Judah. This current leadership was not only very powerful, it was also extremely evil. Knowing this Jehu may have decided acting on this word would have been too hard. He could have easily partnered with the lies that he was too weak, not strong enough, not smart enough and that he was no match for them. I love how much I can relate to this.

Thankfully Jehu was surrounded by fellow army officers who had a high respect for the Elijah the prophet of Yahweh. After Elijah's messenger anointed Jehu the king of Israel and ran off, Jehu's fellow army officers, seeing Jehu dripping in oil, insisted on knowing what happened.

"When Jehu went out to his fellow officers, one of them asked him,
'Is everything all right? Why did this maniac come to you?'

'You know the man and the sort of things he says,' Jehu replied.
'That's not true!' they said. 'Tell us.'
Jehu said, 'Here is what he told me: 'This is what the Lord says: I
anoint you king over Israel.''
They quickly took their cloaks and spread them under him on the
bare steps. Then they blew the trumpet and shouted, 'Jehu is king!''
2 Kings 9:11-13 (NIV)

Notice Jehu's first response is to try to play it "cool" in front of
his friends. "You know the man and the sort of things he says." It
very well could be he was afraid of what his friends may think of his
word and new anointing. Jehu clearly valued his relationship with
these men and did not want anything to come between them.
However, his fellow army officers, his friends, had a high respect for
the prophet of Yahweh and knew immediately there was something
more. Jehu was literally dripping with oil and the messenger had just
run away *like a maniac*. This was not something to ignore or to take
casually. They urged Jehu for the truth. After Jehu shared what the
messenger had said the other army officers did not respond out of
jealousy or anger, but they heard and accepted the word from the
Lord and took immediate action by spreading out their cloaks,
blowing the trumpets and shouting, "Jehu is king."

Let's not overlook how incredibly important it is that we
surround ourselves with an inner group of friends who have a high
respect for Yahweh and His Word. Knowing the Word and speaking
the Word has power especially when the situation seems incredibly
unfavorable. Jehu's friends heard the word of the Lord, and then
spoke it back to him repeatedly. In fact the scripture says they
"shouted." This is significant to note because it wasn't until Jehu's
friends took action on the word and shouted the Word back to him
that Jehu, himself, gained the strength and motivation to put the
word into action.

Remember, there was already a king in Israel: King Joram. So it
wasn't like Israel was lacking a king; Israel was lacking a *godly king*.

King Joram was evil and His mother was worse. Operating under a demonic spirit, she was manipulative, cunning and wicked. With this in mind, Jehu couldn't just walk into the country's capital, announce the Lord has anointed him King, have King Joram respectfully step down and all the people happily start following Jehu. No, this was going to be hard. This was going to be incredibly hard. Acting on this word was declaring war on the evil powers of this dark world.

On his own Jehu may never have taken action on this word, but he was surrounded by people who reinforced the word and Jehu, then made the personal choice to take responsibility for the word and take action. A word from God comes with an anointing, and Jehu's personal choice to align his *will* with God's *will* took out some of the most wicked power houses this world has ever seen.

You might be wondering, how does this relate to our current relationship with our mothers'? If you don't already see it let me explain. When we choose to *surrender* our *will* to align with the Word of God we take major action steps against the evil one and toward fulfilling the powerful purpose God has already put in us. As we operate in our God-given authority we tear down demonic strongholds, advance His Kingdom, bring freedom to people and glorify His name. We are called to be free and do mighty things in the name of Jesus. We can choose to break free from the bondages of our emotionally abusive mother by *surrendering* our *will* to align with God's will. As we do this we get a front row seat to watch how Yahweh increases our ministry and impact for His Kingdom.

Ride Like Jehu

Returning to the story of Jehu, we read, after his friends and fellow officers shouted the Word back to Jehu, in agreement, Jehu set in his heart to surrender his will to the Word of the Lord and take action on the Word.

"Jehu said, 'If you desire to make me king, don't let anyone slip out

of the city to go and tell the news in Jezreel.' Then he got into his
chariot and rode to Jezreel, because Joram was resting there and
Ahaziah king of Judah had gone down to see him.
When the lookout standing on the tower in Jezreel saw Jehu's
troops approaching, he called out, 'I see some troops coming.'
'Get a horseman,' Joram ordered. 'Send him to meet them and ask,
'Do you come in peace?''
The horseman rode off to meet Jehu and said, 'This is what the king
says: 'Do you come in peace?''' 2 Kings 9: 16-18a (NIV)

As part of the plan to carry out the word of the Lord Jehu and his
troops are charging unwaveringly toward Jezreel for the epic, historic
battle to wipe out the wicked leadership of King Joram, his mother
Jezebel and King Ahaziah. This mad, determined charge causes
alarm in Jezreel, and King Joram sends out a horseman to ask Jehu if
he comes in peace. This is interesting because I believe Joram knew
full well by the way Jehu was riding that Jehu was not coming in
peace.

Anyway, the horseman still rides out and when he reaches Jehu
he asks if Jehu comes in peace, as he was instructed to. I love Jehu's
response:

'''What do you have to do with peace?' Jehu replied.
'Fall in behind me.'
The lookout reported, 'The messenger has reached them,
but he isn't coming back.'
So the king sent out a second horseman. When he came to them he
said, 'This is what the king says: 'Do you come in peace?'
Jehu replied, 'What do you have to do with peace?
Fall in behind me.'
The lookout reported, 'He has reached them, but he isn't coming
back either. The driving is like that of Jehu son of Nimshi — he
drives like a maniac.''' 2 Kings 9:18b-20 (NIV)

"What do you have to do with peace?" Jehu replied. "Fall in behind me." So many thoughts are flooding into my mind right now that can be applied to our healing journeys. This horseman is representing a very demonic leadership, ruling its people through manipulation and maintaining control through mind games. This is emotional abuse. This horseman then asks Jehu if he comes in peace. Jehu doesn't even say, "No," he replies with, "What do you have to do with peace?" There is no peace in the kingdom of darkness. There is no peace in leadership operating under a demonic spirit. There is no peace, therefore how do you make peace with a kingdom that has no peace? You can't! Jehu's answer was brilliant. Yet the deception is that there is peace or *could* be peace.

By the horseman asking the question about peace naturally our minds would think the horseman wouldn't ask for peace if it wasn't a possibility. Also we as humans innately know peace is good. We all want peace. In peace there is freedom and rest. If there is a way to make peace, yes, let's do it. This concept of seeking peace is not new to us. However, in a demonically ruled kingdom the concept of peace is distorted and true peace is unknown by the people. As a result, offers of peace can be used to deceive us back into control by the enemy, the devil, preventing us from fulfilling the purpose we were designed for.

Jehu had a word from the Lord to be king and to drive out the evil in the land. Nowhere in that word did the Lord say, "If there is an offer of peace, take it." I repeat, there is no peace in a kingdom operating under demonic spirits. This offer of peace was a mind game the enemy was inviting Jehu to play.

To the enemy's demise, Jehu did not accept the invitation; he didn't even take the time to think about it. Jehu knew there was no peace in that land and he further knew the horseman knew nothing of true peace. The horseman, like many others living in this demonic kingdom, had been manipulated and controlled by evil spirits, possibly his whole life. Jehu was not playing games, and he called for the horseman to make an immediate choice: join Yahweh's army or die. We are to never make peace, play games, or entertain the kingdom of darkness, the evil, manipulating spirits in this world.

Relating this biblical story to myself, I can quickly recall many times when false peace was offered; I took the offer only to be stabbed in the back and hurt again. I was deceived. The world operating outside of God's boundaries does not know true peace. I have learned the hard way to never base a decision about a "peace offering" solely on the offer itself, no matter how enticing the offer is. You always look at the person. What is their reputation? Where is their allegiance? What is the Holy Spirit saying about them?

In my relationship with my mother there was seldom peace. I exhausted myself trying to make peace with her only to get repeatedly sucked back into the same sick cycle of emotional abuse, feeling stabbed in the back and trapped in my miserable life. It was through the study of Jehu I realized there is no making peace with a person who is operating under a demonic spirit. They do not know peace; they want control. It was through studying Jehu I came to the revelation that my struggle with my mother is far beyond dealing with an incredibly difficult person, rather I was fighting with demonic spirits.

I cannot count how many times it appeared my mother was offering peace, only to discover it was just another one of her manipulative tactics and mind games to keep her control over me. Now I understand she was operating under a demonic spirit and she didn't know it. Emotionally abusive mothers are not a part of God's original plan. It is a product of sin. We cannot make peace with someone who plays mind games, manipulates, gaslights (makes us question our perception of reality), is passive-aggressive, mocks, criticizes, and makes fun of us.

Jehu gave the horseman one option, "Fall in behind me." The horseman could choose to join the mission for true peace by wiping out the evil leadership of the land or die. Join or die. We see this happen two more times. Joram sent out a second horseman who also chose to fall in behind Jehu. When that horseman didn't return Joram decided to go out himself.

"'Hitch up my chariot,' Joram ordered. And when it was hitched up, Joram king of Israel and Ahaziah king of Judah rode out, each in his own chariot, to meet Jehu. They met him at the plot of ground that had belonged to Naboth the Jezreelite. When Joram saw Jehu he asked, 'Have you come in peace, Jehu?'
'How can there be peace,' Jehu replied, 'as long as all the idolatry and witchcraft of your mother Jezebel abound?'
Joram turned about and fled, calling out to Ahaziah, 'Treachery, Ahaziah!'
Then Jehu drew his bow and shot Joram between the shoulders. The arrow pierced his heart and he slumped down in his chariot.'"
2 Kings 9: 21-24 (NIV)

Jehu had a word and an anointing and chose to be obedient no matter the cost. Jehu chose to surrender his own plans and agenda to follow the word of the Lord. Jehu possibly had to surrender his own opinions about the situation, about his occupational position, about his relationships and about himself. Jehu was so focused on the word of the Lord every tactic the enemy tried on him to slow him down or stop him failed. Jehu did not stop until the word of the Lord was fulfilled.

In 2 Kings 9 we read the complete fulfillment of the Lord's word: all three evil power houses were killed and Jehu became king of Israel. I love how God's unique and powerful purpose for Jehu was to literally be a king here on earth. God created Jehu with the capability to be a king, and he may not have known it until he received a word from the Lord.

One of our biggest takeaways from the story of Jehu is recognizing that Jehu may never have operated as a king and fulfilled the purpose God created him for if he did not choose to *surrender* his own *will* to align with the word of the Lord. This leads me to ask myself the question *what has God already put in me to fulfill?* I have spent years striving to make things happen for myself. I tried hard to mend my mother and I's relationship on my own. I spent a significant amount of energy trying to find the right path to fulfill my purpose...by myself. I worked hard to escape and ignore my heart wounds to find a joy-filled life.

Trying so hard all the time, there came a moment when I chose to give up and let go. The road to freedom, navigating it on my own, seemed long and the light at the end of the tunnel never seemed to be getting any closer. However, the course of my life shifted when I *surrendered* and cried out to God, "I give up."

Without realizing it my life's course changed. I *surrendered* to God and things began to accelerate in my life in the positive way I had longed for. *Surrendering* my strong *will* to God, my Father and Creator, ended up being the best gift I could ever give myself. In a moment when I expected to feel like a complete failure I never felt more alive, knowing my God has it all under control.

Since then God has brought gifts and abilities out of me I did not know were there. My dream life has increased, both the prophetic and God dreams that come during sleep, and so have my desires of things I would like to see and accomplish. My confidence has increased as well. My confidence is not in myself; it is in who I am *in* and *with* my God, Yahweh.

Give yourself the gift of *surrendering*. Please note when you choose to surrender it is not all candy and rainbows, meaning life will not become all easy and pleasurable. Expect the enemy to come at you, but do not waver; you have a powerful purpose to fulfill. Allow God, our Creator, to show you who you are and bring out things you didn't know were there. Watch your dreams and confidence increase. Let us walk out the Kingdom of Yahweh the way we were created to: fully healed, fully free, and powerfully purposeful queens.

How Do I Surrender?

Surrendering our *will* to align with God's *will* for our lives is allowing God to direct our plans. I have experienced *surrendering* two ways. First, as an encounter with the living God where I throw my hands up in *surrender* to Him, giving up my own ways to follow His. This kind of *surrender* is like crossing the point of no return and fully knowing there is no turning back. The second kind of *surrender* is more on a daily basis, sometimes moment-by-moment, where I intentionally choose to deny my flesh, my *will*, to follow the Holy Spirit. Daily *surrendering* our own plans to God is part of maintaining our relationship with Him.

Throughout my day I continually talk with God, ask Him questions and listen for answers. Sometimes I hear Him clearly, other times I struggle but the struggle never stops me from the desire to be fully *surrendered* to Him. Prayer, continual conversation with God, is the key to maintaining a *surrendered* life to God. Sometimes the prayers are simple, like, "God, help! What do I do?" Other times I am brought to my knees before God, my King, in awe of His glory and power, and I throw my hands up and pour out my heart in complete *surrender*. Sometimes the glory of the Lord falls so powerfully I feel like I can see my life so clearly, almost through the eyes of God Himself. This kind of encounter I find myself questioning why I ever tried to do life on my own apart from His *will*. My conversation with my Father becomes so focused I feel a change happen inside, and I am energized to walk out His *will*, despite the opinions of those around me.

Even as I write this I find myself *surrendering* to the Father. May these writings not be written in vain but used to activate Jehus across the globe; every one of us has been charged to remove evil's crown.

Unboxed Prayer

Father in Heaven, I surrender my will to align with Your will. I am done with feeling stuck on a merry-go-round, going nowhere and experiencing the same hurts, pain and frustrations. I hate feeling like I am not living out who I am created to be. I am done with feeling guilt and shame for who I am. Father, today I am asking that You encounter me in the most powerful way I have ever experienced. I want to be completely changed from the inside out. I surrender all my efforts to better my own life. I give up fighting against the call You have on my life. I give up trying to be who I feel others want me to be. I ask that You activate me in my calling. Set my heart on fire for You. Fill me up with Your joy. Pour out Your courage on me to ride like Jehu, to rule the territory You have given me and to drive out the wickedness in my land. I ask that Your Holy Spirit will guide my every step, because I don't know what I am doing, but I put my trust in You.

In the mighty name of Yeshua, AMEN!

· SIX ·

Heart Posture, My Core

As a child I hated taking family photos. I am sure, anyone in my family could attest to this. My strong dislike of it was made known to everyone. I didn't want to smile. I didn't want to sit up straight. I didn't want to stand or sit closer to my mother. I didn't want to wear the clothes she picked out for me. I hated the way my mother fixed my hair. I didn't want to be there.

The core reason I hated family photos so much was because I felt I was being forced to be someone I wasn't...a happy member of a happy family. We were not a happy family, and I always hated faking it for the world. There was no authenticity in these family photos. So many times I thought of my family as the "whitewashed tombs" Jesus spoke of in Matthew that look beautiful on the outside, but on the inside they are stinky and rotting.

Even though I hated how family photos made me feel I am not justifying my attitude. My attitude during family photos was super stinky and most likely very embarrassing for my parents in front of photographers. I probably should have been embarrassed too, but I was too busy feeling sorry for myself. What stands out to me in this particular memory is how clearly it reveals the posture of my heart. Words and actions reveal who we are as a person.

In the case of family pictures, although my attitude needed an adjustment, I was communicating the only way I knew how that I valued authenticity. Because I didn't feel heard by my parents it was times like family photos when hatred and anger started building up in my heart to cover up the hurt I felt from being forced to perform for the world. As a result, I was deceived into thinking I was protecting my heart from my mother's verbal daggers, but what I was really doing was positioning my heart toward death and away from the purpose I was designed for.

"A good man brings good things out of the good stored up in his heart, and an evil man brings evil things out of the evil stored up in his heart. For the mouth speaks what the heart is full of."
Luke 6:45 (NIV)

What Is A Heart Posture?

The posture of our hearts tells the world around us what kind of person we are on the inside. It can form the core of our being. What we allow to go deep into our hearts ultimately forms its position. If our heart is positioned to be aligned with God's Word, no matter what circumstances or situations we find ourselves in we will be able to stand strong, be confident in who we are and be able to be our true selves representing the Kingdom of Yahweh. If our hearts aren't aligned with God's Word they will always be envious of every person living the life we think we want – a breeding ground for hate, jealousy, anger and bitterness.

The funny thing is when our hearts aren't positioned correctly to be aligned with God's Word we will not be authentic to who God created us to be. I find that funny, because during my bad attitude family photo shoots I truly just wanted to be authentic. But in my protest for the family act I actually forfeited my true self and positioned myself to be unable to be authentic to who I am designed to be.

According to Luke 6:45 the contents of our heart will come out of the mouth. If we hold anger and resentment in our heart we will come across as an angry person. We can try to fake it and put on the "happy" mask the world pressures us to put on, but this is an exhausting way to live. In reality we are not fooling anyone. There is so much pressure from the people around us to be a certain way it

104

only takes one word sometimes for us to have an angry outburst. This is definitely true in my case. Once the angry outburst occurs it is easy for me to store more shame and guilt in my already wounded heart, planting more seeds for the next outburst.

This is no way to live. However, this is exactly how I lived with my mother for years. I would forgive and repent, you know, *clean out the house*, but these seeds of guilt and shame would be shoved deep in my heart into the basement. Out of sight, out of mind. My house may have been clean, but the storage places were cluttered. I didn't know my heart wasn't positioned correctly. Positioning my heart, aligning it with God's Word, was the next step in breaking free from the bondages of my emotionally abusive mother.

How Do I Position My Heart?

Earlier I used the analogy of a junk-filled house to describe repentance. Well, positioning our heart is the deep cleaning of that house. We can go into the basement, attic and garage, wherever the stored items are kept, and not just organize the boxes, but we will go through every box, touch every item in every box and ask ourselves if we need to keep it or get rid of it. As we deep clean our heart be prepared to find things in there you completely forgot about and even things you didn't know were there at all. Yet each piece of junk has been preventing us from fully healing, causing us to act and speak in ways we hate and have kept us on an emotional merry-go-round we can't seem to get off. Let's go through our hearts' storage, pitch some boxes and get off the merry-go-round for good.

As we clean out the clutter I will be referring to spirits that reside in these storage places; spirits keeping us in bondage. I am referring to the demonic strongholds. These are spiritual beings who hate God, work for our enemy (the accuser, the devil) with the assignment to destroy us. I believe there are demons assigned to each of us for the purpose of keeping us "stuck" and preventing us from fulfilling our purpose. When we are successful in living out what we are designed for it is good for God and His Kingdom. Of course this means it is not good for the devil and his dark kingdom.

"Be sober [well balanced and self-disciplined], be alert *and* cautious at all times. That enemy of yours, the devil, prowls around like a roaring lion [fiercely hungry], seeking someone to devour. But resist him, be firm in *your* faith [against his attack—rooted, established, immovable], knowing that the same experiences of suffering are being experienced by your brothers and sisters throughout the world. [You do not suffer alone.]" 1 Peter 5:8-9 (AMP)

Also remember that our fight for emotional and mental freedom is NOT a fight against our mother. It is a spiritual fight.

"For our struggle is not against flesh and blood [contending only with physical opponents], but against the rulers, against the powers, against the world forces of this [present] darkness, against the spiritual *forces* of wickedness in the heavenly (supernatural) *places*." Ephesians 6:12 (AMP)

When I really wanted to position my heart to be set on God's Word, and to have an attitude that reflected that, I simply cried out to the Holy Spirit to reveal everything ungodly stored in my heart. Then, I could get rid of it and have my heart filled with the Word of God instead.

"Holy Spirit, come and reveal to me what is hidden in my heart; open my eyes to see everything that should not be there. Give me the courage and strength to deal with each and every stronghold as needed. Let it be done, I am ready! Amen!"

Pleasing Others

The first box Holy Spirit led me to was labeled "Pleasing Others."

We have all had a box like this stored in our hearts at some point, and it needs to be pitched. As I opened this box I found all the things I have collected over the years; all the things I had readily accessible to use depending on the people I was with. I like to be liked so it seems natural to prepare my heart with what I needed to please whatever crowd I found myself in.

Growing up with an emotionally abusive mother I know I learned it was easier to please her than to speak truth and engage in a resolving conversation. I hate conflict, and we probably all do to some degree, but how we have learned to deal with it, I believe, is a mix of personality and how we grew up. In my home conflict was never resolved. There were no healthy conversations with the aim of positive and beneficial outcomes for the family relationships.

If I had a problem I had to keep it to myself. When I tried to voice an issue, my feelings or any opinion that wasn't shared by my mother, the results were less than favorable. It was often taken as an invitation for verbal and emotional abuse. In these experiences I learned to avoid conflict to please others. The message was *if I want to be valued and liked by those around me I need to please them*, and I did so by avoiding all conflict and going along with whatever other people wanted. My priorities got mixed up at such a young age.

Remember, my family did not have relationship-building conversations. Conversations remained shallow, staying within a boundary of safe topics such as weather, food, sports, movies or TV shows, maybe decorating ideas…maybe? Seriously I was making my own conclusions about who I was with no guidance.

Concluding I needed to avoid conflicts to be liked by my own family spilled over into my social life at school, on the playground and even at church. I had subconsciously started to build my Pleasing Others box in my heart and therefore placed an unhealthy importance on being liked rather than having an open attitude, an authentic desire to learn and grow through healthy and respectful conversations.

To give an example, our second Christmas as a married couple, my husband and I planned to spend the holidays with my parents since the previous Christmas we had spent with His family. I talked to my mother about spending Christmas with them, and she seemed to expect it. My husband and I made plans to drive our car there even though it was a sixteen-hour drive.

I remember my husband being firm with me about driving so we could have our own vehicle. He made clear: no matter what my mother said we were driving. I informed him my mother hadn't said anything, but he knew. He had witnessed my mother manipulate me into doing things I didn't want to do, only to see me end up feeling hurt and betrayed. He now had years of watching her manipulation and control, and he could call it before it happened. He was right.

My mother's calls started coming regularly, voicing how our choice to drive was an unacceptable form of transportation. She first insisted that we fly. We said, "No, we have chosen to drive." She then insisted that we take the train. Again we politely reminded her of our decision to drive. When this didn't work she offered to pay for our trip if we chose to different form of transportation. My mother was persistent. My husband stood strong, but I was starting to wear down.

One day when my husband wasn't home with me I was talking to my mother again about our holiday transportation. She asked why I wouldn't take her offer to pay for another form of transportation. I explained how we wanted the ability to use a vehicle in case we wanted to go somewhere, anywhere – shopping, skating, visiting friends, a winter adventure. We didn't want to be stuck at her house for two weeks. Would anyone really? In response, my mother offered her own vehicle. She said, "Let's compromise. You and your husband can drive part way, park your vehicle and I will buy you train tickets for the rest of the way here. That way you won't be driving as long, you can rest a bit before arriving and when you get here you can use my vehicle."

Everything in me was screaming, "NO!" I knew my husband would be upset if I gave in, but I was worn down. The harassment from my mother about our decision had weakened my stand. I confirmed with her that we could use her vehicle if I agreed to this, and she said, "Yes." I reluctantly reached into my heart and pulled out my Please Others box. I decided it would be easier to please her and do what she wanted than to endure any more of her exhausting manipulating schemes. I didn't want to talk to her on the phone any more. I felt so defeated.

When my gracious husband returned home and I shared the agreement I had made he was not happy. He wasn't angry, but disappointed. I told him she promised us her vehicle. He shook his head. He knew I was tricked again. He knew I walked into a web completely controlled by my mom. I tried to stay positive and say this time may be different. He just said, "We will see."

Unfortunately my husband was right. We spent most of our two-week Christmas vacation stuck at my parents' house. When we arrived, we found out that my dad didn't take time off work to spend with us. He just had the usual Christmas Day and New Year's Day. My mom only took a few days off. My spirit sank. They knew for months I was coming to visit, with their only grandchild, and they didn't take time off to spend with us. My heart was so hurt.

Furthermore, my mom had no intention of actually letting us use her vehicle. When I reminded her of her promise to me on the phone, she claimed she agreed to let us use it only a few times, with restrictions. We felt so controlled by her. Needless to say we had a horrible time. We enjoy being out and about, exploring and adventuring. Yet, we were stuck in a house that was not ours and spent a lot of time alone.

I still remember my husband sharing with me he knew this would happen. I humbled myself to say he was right. Pleasing my mom was prioritized above my husband, and I was wrong. I thought I was keeping the peace by living out of my Please Others box, but I was wrong. I had allowed my mother a foothold in my marriage, and that was wrong. I didn't know what to do. *How do I stop living out of my Please Others box?* I didn't know how to live in true peace or what true peace really was. Growing up I certainly didn't learn it. I didn't know my heart was positioned so poorly, and I didn't know how to fix it.

Before moving on, I just want to say my husband has never been truly angry with me when I walk into another one of my mother's traps. He tries to guide me through it and sees it as a learning opportunity and doesn't allow me to beat myself up over it. He has been the most patient with me and my biggest cheerleader in my healing journey. He is not afraid to redirect me or help me learn how to have those honest conversations. He approaches conversations about my healing with a curiosity to learn and a great respect for who I am as a child of God. He has never been insistent I hear his voice. He truly models hearing what is being said first before speaking. I never had that modeled for me before.

This memory used to be accompanied by sadness, guilt and shame. Now I choose to speak love into this memory, and I see the love so clearly through my husband. I love that this was a learning opportunity to shift how I respond in life and relationships. Where was Jesus? I see him in my husband, who never left me, walked with me through it and loved and valued me every moment.

The "Please Others" Box

"For where your treasure is, there your heart will be also."
Matthew 6:21 (ESV)

Let us not align our hearts to please the people around us. We will never be able to please everyone because we were not created to. During Jesus' famous *Sermon on the Mount* He invites us to examine our hearts by saying, "For where your treasure is, there your heart will be also." What we treasure in our hearts becomes what we worship. We were designed by our Creator, Elohim, to worship Him, to please Him. He created us for His purposes, not the purposes of man. If we find we have this box tucked away in our hearts we must pitch it and get our hearts to agree with the truth: we don't need to please anyone...just Him. When the opinions of others are above the opinions of our King in our heart He is robbed of our worship because we give it to the idol of Please Others.

Also, pleasing others is not a value we see operating in the Kingdom of God. If you are a citizen of Heaven (because you accepted Jesus as King of your life) we look to the Gospels to read about the life and teaching of Yeshua. He is the model of how to live life here on Earth as citizens of Heaven. Nowhere in the Gospels do we see Yeshua modeling or teaching the lifestyle of Pleasing Others. If we do not get this box out of our heart we will constantly feel obligated to please others and doing so can destroy our future.

When I die the opinions of others will not matter. They will have no weight. So why should I spend the majority of my time pleasing others and glorifying their opinions at the expense of storing up treasures in Heaven and forfeiting the life I was created for? It is not random that the enemy snuck this box in my heart. My need to feel liked and valued is real and significant. The deception is that I need to fill this desire myself by pleasing those around me and manipulating them into liking me using the tactics I collected in this box. The truth is, all I need is found in Christ. I do not need to please others. I need to spend time with the Holy Spirit and allow Him to fill me and meet this need.

Poverty Mindset

The next box Holy Spirit led me to open from my heart's storage unit is titled "Poverty Mindset." When I was first led to this box I wasn't quite sure what a Poverty Mindset was. With guidance from the Holy Spirit I learned that the poverty mindset is simply the strong belief I will never have enough. It leads me to a negative attitude toward money and nice things and convinces me that seeking wealth is ungodly. It had caused me to self-sabotage and demolished any dream of financial success.

God revealed that for me it was more than just believing I would never have enough money; I truly believed I didn't *deserve* to have enough money. Not only is this mindset tied to not deserving enough money, but not deserving to be successful in a career that would earn me enough money. The lie that I am undeserving comes up again, revealing how deeply it is rooted in my heart.

As a result of this poverty mindset I always played it safe with my finances, my job choices and honestly many other areas of my life including relationships. It was like I adopted the motto, "Don't shoot for the stars when the tree is comfortable." Looking back on my life I see many areas where the poverty mindset was at the forefront of my decisions, steering me away from where I really wanted to go. It convinced me I didn't deserve it or couldn't afford it, and therefore should settle for another option I believed was more for me.

The biggest example that comes to mind is my education. I really wanted to attend a certain university but convinced myself I could never afford it, so I chose a cheaper option: a college which I felt fit me more. That particular college experience wasn't the greatest. I didn't leave that school feeling accomplished or even proud to be a graduate of that school. Too many times I have regretted going there. However, God knew I would settle for this college, and I truly believe I was meant to attend there for one year, just not all four.

There was definitely favor on that first year. I met my husband, a prophecy from years early was fulfilled and I grew spiritually. The next three were tough. But since I had this poverty mindset I did not feel I deserved to transfer to the school I really wanted to go to.

The poverty mindset caused me to limit my dreams. Whenever I began to dream of a greater career and financial success, this mindset kicked in and reminded me I wasn't deserving of such a dream. How did this box get in my heart? I believed a lie from the evil one. This lie was rooted in comments and actions by both my mother and my father. I honestly believe my parents' intentions were good, however the evil one distorted the message they were trying to convey, and I unknowingly partnered with a lie. Through this distorted message I began to believe I could not be financially successful on my own.

As a child my mother had a huge influence on how I spent my money (as parents should). However, some of my mother's financial influence impacted me quite negatively. I do not believe she purposefully did it. Reflecting on various incidences I truly believe it was all subconscious but intentionally schemed by the devil.

For example, each year I got birthday money and my mother would make strong suggestions on how I should spend it. I remember one year she was so insistent I spend my money a certain way even though I didn't want to. I bought what she suggested to please her. Feeling sad that I spent all my birthday money on something I didn't really want, I was convinced pleasing her was the better option.

As I reflect on this I wonder if this is where the seeds for my poverty mindset crept in, making me insecure about my own money management and undermining my own dream of financial success. I certainly don't blame my mother. It was the devil's evil plan. My mother was just the vessel he used.

I have pitied myself in the area of finances and success and found I became jealous of others who were financially successful. I would focus on what I didn't have but didn't make any real goals to attain more either because I felt undeserving. The poverty mindset is another sick cycle and another box I needed to pitch. My God, Yahweh, my King, is the One who decides who is deserving and who is not. He is the One who will lead me into financial favor.

In one of his on-line teachings Michael Dalton said, "Nothing can limit you unless you agree to be limited." This sentence hit me hard and has stuck with me. The depth of truth in this one little sentence is still being unpacked. If God has not limited me in the area of finances, then why should I limit myself?

The Poverty Mindset box, as well as many other boxes we will find in the storage places of our hearts, limit us where we were not meant to be limited. God doesn't have limits and neither does His

Kingdom. If you have accepted Christ as Lord and Savior you are a part of the limitless Kingdom and should never agree to be limited by anything not of the Kingdom. This means we need to change our mindset, our thoughts, towards money. If you are a part of this Kingdom your finances have no limits, and your success in any area of your life has no limits.

Orphan Mindset

As I continue to position my heart to align with truth I dive deeper into the storage unit and unpack a box labeled "Orphan Mindset." It's another mindset I didn't even know was there. In fact it is only as I write this book the Lord has revealed to me a new layer of what this mindset is. I had heard the term Orphan Mindset before, but I didn't know what it meant or that it applied to me. Well, to my surprise it does. As I brush the dust off this hidden junk, explore with me the disheartening contents of this Orphan Mindset box.

First, an orphan mindset doesn't mean you are literally orphaned, as in both your parents died or you were abandoned. In my research I found an on-line article where Mike Bachelder provides a great definition: "The orphan mindset is a pattern of thinking that often goes back to childhood. It has to do with thoughts, as well as emotions. If we continue in this mindset, it becomes a stronghold. This is a fortified citadel in our soul where the enemy dominates our thinking, emotions and self-perceptions."

This definition is eye opening for me. It reveals a very specific stronghold the devil has had in my life, preventing me from living the passionate life I feel so abundantly in my soul. The scary part is this stronghold was set up deep in my heart as a child, and I just discovered it was there two weeks ago (from time of writing). WHAT!? The scarier part is the very people God has designed to protect us as children are the very people the devil uses as vessels to set up demonic strongholds before we even reach an age of understanding.

I truly believe every victim of emotional abuse has this Orphan Mindset box tucked away in the storage places of their heart. It is through this stronghold our enemy, Satan, the devil, tries to control our thinking, emotions and our perception of ourselves. Yikes!

The orphan mindset is part of the reason I have found it difficult to receive love from others. Love in my relationship with my mother always felt so conditional and her words felt empty. Without knowing it my belief that love was conditional became a part of my pattern of thinking. I learned I had to earn love. I also created the belief that in order to feel love I needed to feel I deserved it. Therefore, hearing the words "I love you" from anyone meant nothing to me unless I had decided I deserved to hear them (which I never actually did). I truly believed I didn't deserve anyone's love.

This revelation is hitting me deeper as I write; I am just now discovering I have subconsciously believed I do not deserve to be loved unless I earn it. For years I have walked away from very loving people, only to leave myself wondering why later.

Remember the co-worker I mentioned who hugged me and said, "I don't know why your mom doesn't love you"? That wonderful woman loved on me with her big heart and wide-open arms. She wanted to stand in the gap for the aching heart I didn't know I had. She saw what I needed before I knew I needed it. Yet some part of me got scared, and I did not know why until now. When I moved away for college I allowed the distance to keep us apart even though she assured me I could call any time to talk. There were so many times I wished I had called, and so many times I wondered if I hurt her by not receiving the love she was pouring out. I now see I felt I didn't deserve her love, and so I ran.

Another example comes to mind when a beautiful couple from a church my husband and I went to loved on us and wanted to mentor us as a young couple. At first I was excited because I longed to have a mother figure in my life. I felt so lonely raising children without a mother figure guiding and helping me. The more love this amazing woman poured out on me, inviting me to join her family for various functions, bringing dinner for my family when I was unable to cook, helping us get our house ready to sell, and being someone I could call for anything at any time, somewhere along the way I got scared and just stopped calling.

Due to my orphan mindset I did not feel accepted and internally had the need to get attention. I strongly felt I was not accepted in my family especially by my mother. However, my need to gain attention from her was masked. My attempts to gain my mother's attention throughout childhood, teen years and even early adult years were subconscious. I would act out in unfavorable ways in the home which would get me in trouble or punished. I remember not knowing why I would throw fits or behave poorly in front of her. It wasn't the real me, and I didn't act like this outside of her presence. I hated the way I acted around her and always experienced guilt for the behavior I felt I couldn't control.

Now I understand my orphan mindset was subconsciously trying to fulfill my desperate need for attention. As a result, I was behaving a way that made me stand out to her. The little girl me was screaming not only for her attention, but for her to see me, love me, want me.

While still trying to gain my mother's attention through poor behavior, somewhere along the way I concluded I didn't belong with her or my family. I would often share with people that I was the white sheep in a family of black sheep. I know the saying goes "black sheep of the family," but I refused to believe I was the odd one out. By saying I was the white sheep I was communicating that I believed there was something wrong with all of them, not me. Which I know isn't true.

For real though, I didn't feel like I belonged. The orphan mindset created feelings that I did not belong, and I often questioned why God put me in the family He did, especially with my mother. Feeling like I didn't belong with my family caused me to detach emotionally, not just from my family, but from everyone. I also developed an attitude of independence. There was this inner sense of abandonment leading me to mistakenly believe I had to be as independent as I

116

could. This mindset caused me to push a lot of very loving people in my life away or keep them at an arms-length; people I actually really needed in my life.

Rummaging a little more in this Orphan Mindset box I find pieces of fear and insecurity. It is true, not feeling like I belonged in my own family caused me to question if I really belonged *anywhere*. Whether in the work place, school, in church or in a family I never truly found where I belonged. I was independent, abandoned, hurt and scared of being hurt more.

Without knowing it I became extremely protective of my heart. I became so good at protecting my heart from further damage I had become incredibly insecure. In almost every setting I felt vulnerable and unprotected. I lacked confidence in who I was, who God had made me to be, and therefore feared never being good enough anywhere. Places where I wanted to fit in, like at church or work, I felt the need to prove myself over and over again. Once I felt I had proven myself, then I craved the approval of leadership.

The approval of leadership was a must in order to keep going in that position with the same energy I'd started with. When I didn't receive the recognition or approval I was seeking I became discouraged, felt I didn't fit in or I didn't belong there either and started planning my exit. If I didn't belong, I didn't want to stay. Growing up in a home where I felt I didn't belong was painful, and I didn't need nor did I want to relive that experience if I didn't have to. This was one way I protected my sore, wounded heart.

The habits, attitudes and thinking patterns the orphan mindset developed were destructive and I didn't even know it. They were preventing me from being who my Creator designed me to be and living my passionate joy-filled life. I was deceived. Thinking I was protecting myself I was actually preventing myself from embracing who I was. By keeping others at arms-length I hadn't realized I also was keeping my Creator at arms-length. I wasn't letting Him in to show me who I was. I had been fed lies about my very nature my whole life, and I had a loving Father in Heaven, my Creator, longing to show me who He created me to be. Even so I was too afraid and remained emotionally detached from Him as well.

The habits, attitude and thinking patterns I had subconsciously formed to protect me were destroying me. They were my way of survival in this dark, cruel world. But what I was using as a way of survival was actually killing me from the inside out. Screaming to be rescued because the orphan mindset was slowly sucking the life out of me, I simultaneously never trusted anyone enough to rescue me. Again, deep down, I believed I didn't deserve it.

Rejection

Next to the Orphan Mindset box on the same storage shelf in my heart I found a box labeled "Rejection." I already knew the Rejection box was there; this one was no surprise. In fact it is still a sore spot the devil likes to jab at. The spirit of rejection has taken residence in this box, and somewhere in my life I gave this evil spirit permission to do so. Ever since it moved in rejection has operated through me effectively. The origin of this box was my mother.

Even though I didn't consciously give the spirit of rejection a home in my heart it made its home there anyway when I subconsciously partnered with its lie: I am not enough. Evil spirits do not wait for permission; they see an open door and they enter. Deep down I felt very rejected by my mother. Rejection led me to make the false conclusion, *since my mother rejects me, everyone can and will reject me.*

As a result, raw, tender, deeply painful emotions developed and never went away. These emotions covered me inside like a heavy coat. The intensity in which I felt them varied depending on who I was with and what experiences I was going through. These emotions created a thought pattern, a sort of filter or lens in which I saw (more like judged) "my place" in every area of life, work, school, family, friends, social events, the line at the grocery store, and the list goes on. If there were people I used my emotions from previous rejections as my lens to see the world around me. This wrong mindset prevented me from being confident in who I was made to be.

My emotional lens was actually a subconscious defense mechanism to guard my heart and avoid re-experiencing the deep pain of rejection. Rejection inhabited my heart for as long as I can remember. I am brought to tears thinking about how much of my life has been robbed because I failed to see the world through the eyes of my Creator. So much time was spent feeling very lonely because being lonely was better than risking rejection. I felt like I was the only one experiencing judgment from every person around me in every situation. This is how rejection made me feel, but it is not the truth.

The truth is every person has experienced rejection in some way, shape or form. It is something all humans experience and it is something all humans feel isolated in at some point. As I reflect on my box labeled "Rejection" I want you to know we have all been there. No one is alone in this. However, each of us choose how we respond to this box now and in the future.

Let's ask ourselves this question: "How is rejection working in my life right now and what am I going to do about it?" Reflect on your life right now. Have you made any decisions today through the lens of rejection?

Mary the mother of Jesus, the most famous woman in history, is an amazing example of how we can handle rejection. Many of you are well aware of the story of Mary the mother of Jesus, however for this point I will briefly recap. Mary was a young virgin who was engaged to be married to Joseph. One day God sent the angel Gabriel to Mary with a life-changing message. Gabriel greeted her with, "Greetings, you who are highly favored! The Lord is with you" (Luke 1:28 NIV). Taken back by seeing an angel Mary didn't know what to think. Gabriel assured her she didn't need to be afraid and repeated to her that she had found favor with the Lord. From there he did not waste time and gave her the message from the Lord. The message was she would become pregnant with a baby while still a virgin, and that baby would be called Yeshua. Further, Yeshua would be the Son of the Most High God.

Mary asked Gabriel how this could even be possible, since in our earthly understanding virgins can't become pregnant. Gabriel reminds her, "For no word from God will ever fail" (Luke 1:37 NIV). Mary's response is key:

"'I am the Lord's servant,' Mary answered. 'May your word to me be fulfilled.' Then the angel left her." Luke 1:38 (NIV)

For Mary to respond the way she did she would have had to have great trust in the Lord. She completely trusted the Lord to use her the way He chose to. Putting her complete trust in the Lord in this way she gave up all of herself: her body, her comfort, possibly her relationships and her reputation. She clearly had high respect for the word of the Lord and was more concerned about her obedience to her Lord than her image to her community. In case you are not aware of the problem with this pregnancy...Mary was a virgin. She had never had sex with her fiancé Joseph. Joseph knew this baby was not his, therefore in the natural realm the baby belongs to another man, meaning Mary had committed adultery. Committing adultery is breaking one of the Ten Commandments and is punishable by death. Mary was quite literally giving up her own life to obey the word of the Lord.

With the title *adulterer* possibly hanging over Mary many people she may have loved dearly could have been completely offended, disgusted or even hurt by her growing belly. Yeshua was already being rejected before He was even born. But that is not the direction I am going here. Let's keep our eyes on Mary and imagine the possible rejection she may have felt from the only community she had ever known – her own family, friends and neighbors. All these people may have treated her differently, maybe unkindly, making her feel alone and rejected.

When the world around Mary judged her based on unfound evidence, on presumptions, on gossip, she still chose to believe the word of the Lord. I wonder if she would lie awake at night after a rough day of enduring rejection and repeat these words to herself, "I am highly favored. I am blessed by my Lord." You see, in the midst of rejection Mary chose to believe His word over the words of anyone else.

Let's follow Mary's example; have confidence in the Word of our Lord, trust Him with all of our being. Stop looking at the world through the wrong lenses. Stop judging our place in a room through our emotions. Stop rejecting ourselves, thinking we are protecting our hearts from the pain of another rejection. Yeshua, who was already judged and rejected in His mother's womb, died on the cross so that we can be free. Even if our mothers didn't want us from the time we were conceived in the womb Yeshua understands and He died because He wanted us. We are worth it to Him. Rejection is nailed to that cross. Rejection may have been a part of our identity up until now, but today is the day to recognize that our identity is in Yeshua and we are who God our Creator says we are. We are not rejected. We are fully accepted by our God, and He is the only One who matters. Shout out these truths with me:

I am chosen, "God chose us to belong to Christ before the world was created. He chose us to be holy and without blame in his eyes. He loved us." Ephesians 1:4 (NIRV)

I am a child of God! "Now you are no longer a slave but God's own child. And since you are his child, God has made you his heir." Galatians 4:7 (NLT)

I am His, called by name! "Do not be afraid, for I have ransomed you. I have called you by name; you are mine." Isaiah 43:1b (NLT)

I am SO loved! "The Lord appeared to us in the past, saying: 'I have loved you with an everlasting love; I have drawn you with unfailing kindness.'" Jeremiah 31:3 (NIV)

Don't let rejection destroy your future. This box has not only been pitched into the trash, I am crushing it and tearing it to bits as I throw it in.

False Humility

Another box I found tucked away in my heart's storage was "False Humility." I had read the term False Humility many times before in the Bible and from the pulpit, yet never stopped to ponder what it actually was or considered it may have found its way into my heart. It had, however, and was sneaking out in some very big and unexpected ways.

Before I entered this journey of positioning my heart to be aligned with God's Word I would think about false humility as a person who would continuously brag about their selfless acts, seeking praise from those around them. We have all known people like that, and we all have rolled our eyes when they once again begin a sentence with, "I don't mean to brag, but..." Really? If you don't mean to brag, then just keep your mouth shut. I wasn't one of these people, was I? I mean, I would never consider myself a huge bragger, at least not vocally.

Diving into this False Humility box in my heart I found myself asking if I had become one of *those* people who I don't like and try to avoid. I didn't see myself like that, but I knew this box was here in my heart for a reason; I needed to find out how false humility was operating in my life.

Reflecting on false humility I am reminded of when Yeshua Jesus surrendered his life on the cross; He died for all my sin and all my bondage so I may be fully free to be who I was created to be. When I accepted Yeshua as my Lord and Savior I accepted His gift of the cross, including the freedom from every bondage. Therefore, I do not have to live in bondage or operate under any spirit that does not come from my Father in Heaven. This deep cleaning of my heart is like a free junk removal service provided by my Father All I have to do is accept the gift and allow Him access to my heart's storage area, cleaning it out in preparation for the great plans He has for me.

With that said, the Lord revealed some things in my False Humility box I didn't know were there: bitterness, jealousy and pride.

False humility masks pride. The Merriam-Webster dictionary defines pride as "inordinate self-esteem: CONCEIT," and then defines conceit as "excessive appreciation of one's own worth or virtue." With further exploration I find at dictionary.com that pride is defined as "a high or inordinate opinion of one's own dignity, importance, merit, or superiority, whether as cherished in the mind or as displayed in bearing, conduct, etc." What I notice here is a whole lot of focus on someone's *own self.* Whether it is quite vocal or silent pride is very dangerous and destructive. And yet it can be masked so well we don't even know that it is there.

The Lord has shown me I had pride in my ability to see needs and to do everything I could to fulfill them. I easily saw "holes" in churches, workplaces, organizations, etc., such as positions that needed fulfilling in areas of cleaning, planning, or organizing and often took it upon myself to fill them if I knew I could. My pride was unknowingly hurt when the support needed to effectively fill each hole wasn't provided. The false humility I operated in developed a bitterness and jealousy of those who had been promoted in various areas of life, while ignoring the holes I was trying to fill on my own or with very little help. It was here where jealousy and bitterness got masked by false humility along with my pride.

While operating under false humility the Lord further revealed to me that I enjoyed receiving praise and exchanging divisive comments with others who also were operating under this spirit and had experienced similar disappointment.

Real humility surrenders to the will of our Creator, our Father. False humility creates a false identity which leads us to being unsure about ourselves and of the steps we are to be taking in our lives. In this unsureness, this confusion of our identity, we stop fighting for ourselves. We feel defeated and can give up. We have lost who we are and are so unsure of what we are supposed to be doing. Hear me, I am preaching to myself right now.

In my own life I can now clearly see where false humility has crept in. Lost and stuck, I have spent years unsure of the steps I should be taking, what I should be doing, and feeling like I am not allowed to be myself. As a result, I have buried myself in responsibilities that are actually not mine. As I saw needs crop up around me I would volunteer for a gross number of things. When my responsibilities grew and others didn't respond to my multiple cries for assistance I grew bitter. I would convince myself to be content in my miserable volunteering, thinking this is what being a humble servant of the Lord was.

While I was trying to be humble I felt walked over, undervalued, unseen and stuck. Unfortunately this false humility was what I observed from various people around me too, mistakenly thinking this was true humility, meek, weak and content. But I wasn't content.

Does this mean there is something wrong with me? Am I not godly enough? The answer is no. There was nothing wrong with me, I just needed to do some heart cleaning with my Creator, claim my true identity and educate myself on true humility.

A person operating under the spirit of false humility is not living in their true identity. We need to recognize when speaking with a person operating under the spirit of false humility it can feel like they are launching missiles or throwing punches with their words at every person who has failed to validate them in their *selfless* service. Now I see that I have done this myself. Even though it may appear to be words intentionally used for hurting others, they are actually words coming from a place of deep hurt, and this was my attempt, in the only way I knew how, to make myself feel better. I was crying out for someone to make me feel better. I wanted the pain of the jealousy and bitterness to go away. I was trying to navigate my way out of my wilderness where I felt stuck.

Living out of the False Humility box, or rather living while operating under the spirit of false humility, feels like being stuck in the wilderness. Unfortunately many people would rather remain in the desert than navigate their way into their promise. This is because false humility's lie we believe is that staying in our wilderness is the *godliest* thing we can do. We falsely believe this as true humility when it is not. True surrender is knowing who you are in God. Many are stuck in this wilderness because they have not aligned themselves up with the Word of God and have not been obedient to His Word.

Please don't misunderstand me. I know there are strong God-fearing people who go through seasons in the wilderness, such as Paul after his Damascus Road experience and Jesus who had a time of temptation in the wilderness. Many of God's followers in this present age go through seasons of wilderness. There are times when the Lord leads us there, but we are not meant to stay nor are we meant to send ourselves there. If the Lord isn't leading us there the wilderness isn't going to make us more holy. Finally, the wilderness was never meant to become our home or our identity.

We usually don't have to look far to find people who are vocal about their wilderness excursions and stays. Social media, to some, has become a platform for wilderness sharing, looking for people to validate them in their miserable, humble living. These people often talk with zero intensions of finding their way out of the wilderness, as if to share with the world that being content with their wilderness is godly. Letting everyone know how humble you are isn't humility. It's like when people have to explain the joke, the joke isn't funny. If you have to tell people how humble you are, you are not humble.

"Therefore humble yourselves under the mighty hand of God [set aside self-righteous pride], so that He may exalt you [to a place of honor in His service] at the appropriate time, casting all your cares [all your anxieties, all your worries, and all your concerns, once and for all] on Him, for He cares about you [with deepest affection, and watches over you very carefully]." 1 Peter 5:6-7 (AMP)

True humility is powerful. When you know who you are, who you were created to be, your security and confidence is in your Heavenly Father. You don't have to convince yourself to be satisfied in the wilderness and you don't have to feel guilty or ashamed for not feeling content with your wilderness. That isn't humility. The wilderness is there for us to grow in character and to deepen our relationship with our Father in Heaven as we learn to depend on Him as our provider. The wilderness is a necessary place for mental, emotional and spiritual growth, to prove our character, to test our obedience, and to humble us (Deut. 8). However, the wilderness was never intended to be our home.

Even the Israelites wandered in the wilderness; they didn't set up permanent dwelling places there. If you have ever felt like you were being humble or godly by accepting your life in the wilderness that is false humility. You know deep down you are miserable. You know deep down you are jealous of every person who seems to be advancing in life and you feel stuck.

We don't have to be stuck. God has such a rich, powerful plan for our lives. Yeshua knew who He was in the Father. He said that He will only do what He sees His Father do.

"So Jesus answered them by saying, 'I assure you *and* most solemnly say to you, the Son can do nothing of Himself [of His own accord], unless it is something He sees the Father doing; for whatever things the Father does, the Son [in His turn] also does in the same way.'" John 5:19 (AMP)

Jesus knew the Word of God and was completely surrendered to the will of the Father. As a result, He brought about and completed a powerful mission here on earth to advance the Kingdom of God and glorify His Father in Heaven. We are to follow the model Yeshua has set. The key to navigate our way out of the wilderness successfully is by knowing the Word of God, spending time with our Creator and completely surrendering our lives to the will of God and our Father.

In doing so we will find true humility empowers and deepens our relationship with our Heavenly Father and empowers us to complete the work He designed for us to do here on earth.

Can you imagine the enhancement of your prayer life and your walk with God? There is no show, no spot light, no pressure...just pure surrender. I imagine a lioness coming out, not afraid to be bold, and that boldness entering our conversations with the Father, bringing our prayer life to deep and powerful levels we didn't know existed.

Please hear me, I am going through this discovery along with you, and I feel almost giddy just thinking about how bold and courageous I would be in my relationship with God if I truly understood who I was and was able to practice true humility. I am excited. As we step out in boldness, form a deep relationship with His Word, knowing His Word and surrender to His will I believe we will see how truly powerful humility is. We will be so caught up in thinking about our Father, gazing upon His beauty, in awe of His power, we won't be thinking about ourselves.

We will also be so confident in who we are in Him we won't worry about thinking too lowly or highly of ourselves. Maybe we won't be thinking of ourselves at all. We will know who we are and be completely secure in that. Let the Father define us. Let us surrender. Throw this box in the trash and burn it. I am done feeling bitter and jealous on the inside because I have convinced myself that acting humble is the godly thing to do.

The Spirit Of Religion

After discarding the False Humility and burning it I came to my next box labeled "Religion." In this box resides a powerful spirit, targeting the unity of God's people, the spirit of religion. Perhaps it is better understood as a Religious Mindset. I have heard this bondage described both ways, and I do believe they are the same. However, at this time I have chosen to use the term *spirit of religion*.

Also for me there's something helpful about visualizing this as a labeled box, something physical that can be cast out, thrown out and trashed.

The spirit of religion is a close partner of false humility's. If you found the spirit of false humility in your heart, the spirit of religion will be hiding there too. So do not be quick to dismiss the idea of this spirit residing in your heart, keeping you blinded to the bondage it has you in. I know from experience.

I found this great definition of the spirit of religion on the website JustDisciple.com: "The spirit of religion is a shift from joyful obedience in God and a transformed life, to simply doing the right things and abstaining from the wrong ones. The spirit of religion only allows for outward righteousness. It does not transform the person or the heart. Rather, it puts on a front and appearance that is no greater than skin deep."

Earlier I shared how much I had hated family pictures as a child because they felt fake. Those pictures did not accurately represent our family. Sometimes I wonder what people actually saw when they saw my family or my mother. Did they see past my mother's "happy" family portraits? Did people see the real us? If so, then did they just feel it was safer to play the fake game with us rather than actually engage in our real life? I wonder. What did others really see?

I may never know how the world truly saw my family, but I do know we were not alone in hiding behind a fabricated outward appearance. Let's be honest. My mother was not and is not the only one who has tried to keep up a happy family front to the world. We have all been there, done that. This spirit has been passed down for generations. We have seen it in movies, with our neighbors, our friends and even ourselves.

Facebook hasn't been nicknamed "Fakebook" for no reason. It feels as though some people only post all the fun, cute and perfect things their family or they have done, yet on the inside many of us have been suffering silently with depression, anxiety, stress, self-discipline, laziness, disobedience, etc. I know the list can go on for all of us.

The question is where did all this pressure come from to look good to the world while allowing ourselves to suffer in silence? Well, as I finished writing the question the Lord almost instantly reminded me of the Garden of Eden. Even with small questions the Lord is listening and ready to give an answer. Our God is so good.

I laugh to myself as I think of the problem of Fakebook originating in a garden thousands of years ago. Yet when we read in the Bible about the fall of man I can see it. Eve was deceived into thinking she could make herself better than the perfect creation God had already made her to be. In that moment of temptation Eve doubted the word of God and put herself above that word. After giving in to the temptation and eating the forbidden fruit she recognized her mistake, covered herself up and hid. Yes, Adam was there too, but I was purposefully focusing on Eve because she is a woman, and I relate to her more.

"But the serpent said to the woman, 'You certainly will not die! For God knows that on the day you eat from it your eyes will be opened [that is, you will have greater awareness], and you will be like God, knowing [the difference between] good and evil.' And when the woman saw that the tree was good for food, and that it was delightful to look at, and a tree to be desired in order to make one wise *and* insightful, she took some of its fruit and ate it; and she also gave some to her husband with her, and he ate. Then the eyes of the two of them were opened [that is, their awareness increased], and they knew that they were naked; and they fastened fig leaves together and made themselves coverings." Genesis 3:4-7 (AMP)

When we put our desires above the Word of God we sever the relationship we were designed to be in. We will never fully enter into the purpose we were designed for outside of a relationship with the Creator. God created us in His image (Gen. 1:27). He knows the plans He has for us (Jer. 29:11). He wants to walk with us (Lev. 26:12). He sent His Son for us (John 3:16). His Son came so we can have life to the fullest (John 10:10). We were meant for relationship, not religion. God did not send His Son to this world to establish a new religion. NO! God sent His Son to earth to live, love and die to restore the relationship with us that was lost that day in the Garden of Eden. That day, known as The Fall, religion began to take the place of our relationship with God. It began with doubt, and then continued with a covering, attempting to make ourselves look righteous without God.

The spirit of religion is our attempt to make ourselves look better, and maybe feel better too, by creating an appearance that is not authentic. In order to maintain this desired appearance we create standards and rules for ourselves to follow. When we follow these standards and rules religiously we ignore God's Word and successfully operate under the spirit of religion.

I believe this is a problem, a spirit, that has been passed down from prior generations. My family was not the exception. My mother was no different in this area than other mothers, and I am no different either. I can honestly say I have held some unspoken standards in my life that weren't biblical, but I followed them as if they were. This isn't right, nor is it normal. Just because we can look around us, or look to any social media platform, and see everyone putting on a front, it doesn't mean this is the way it was meant to be. It wasn't! This is not our original design. Mothers were not created to be the masters of disguise for their families. Our calling is so much higher.

I say all this to make a point. This box in my heart with the Spirit of Religion may have been inherited. If I wasn't born with it, it found its way in at a very young age, unintentionally, through my mother. She also may have inherited it as an unhealthy desire to be accepted and valued by her community for appearing a specific way (as if our value comes from a community).

Why are we under the false assumption that we have to impress our community or make ourselves look better than everyone else in it? Life isn't a competition as some may think. Making ourselves and our family look as righteous as possible does not win us points. We can be the family that looks like they have it all together, but guess what? The goal of life is not to be the envy of the community. This is why this spirit is so dangerous and destructive. It has torn the body of Christ apart repeatedly throughout history, and it will continue to do so unless we rebuke this spirit if religion and follow the Word of God as our only agenda.

The spirit of religion divides us when the extra biblical standards and rules we put on ourselves to maintain a righteous appearance are pushed on those around us. When others do not follow our standards and rules to our specifications or liking ugly separations can and have happened. This has happened on a large scale (church separation) and small (friendship or family breakups). Seriously, where do any of us get off thinking we are better or more righteous than the next person? The only reason we have any righteousness at all is because of the work Jesus did on the cross and receiving His amazing gift of salvation.

When we operate under the spirit of religion we are not connecting with God and cannot genuinely connect with each other. Oh my God! I hated our family portraits because it was a representation of a connectedness that wasn't there. I saw my mother as the master of disguise, when in reality as mothers we are all called to be masters of connectedness, leading our families to connect to the heart of the Father. Then, as a result we will naturally connect with each other. What if it is innate for women to be connectors? But without the knowledge, training or insight needed we might try to make connections, not with the wrong things, but in the wrong order. As citizens of a heavenly Kingdom we need to stick to the script laid out for us and pay special attention to its order.

"But first *and* most importantly seek (aim at, strive after) His Kingdom and His righteousness [His way of doing and being right—the attitude and character of God], and all these things will be given to you also." Matthew 6:33 (AMP)

Let me break this down. In the Bible Matthew 6 explains that we first need to seek the Kingdom of God and His righteousness. The Kingdom of God is the rule and reign of Yeshua Jesus here on earth. Yeshua is not only the Son of God, but He IS God. Jesus said in John 10:30 "**I and the Father are One** [in essence **and** nature]" (AMP). Jesus also said, "I am the [only] Way [to God] and the [real] Truth and the [real] Life; no one comes to the Father but through Me" (John 14:6 AMP). Therefore, we are able to conclude the only way to know and connect to the heart of the Father is to know His Son, Yeshua, Jesus.

We do this by consciously and deliberately connecting to Jesus in a personal relationship through prayer, meditating on the Word of God, studying and reading the Word, writing the Word on our own hearts (scripture memorization), walking and talking with Him, and daily surrendering to His will. Through this meaningful relationship with Jesus we seek His Kingdom and His righteousness first above everything else in our lives.

It is here where we break through the spirit of religion – no more making ourselves appear righteous on the outside. This is not our role. We do not get to create our own way of doing and being right. We are to connect to Jesus and seek His righteousness. It is not wrong to desire to look righteous to the people around us. We actually are created to look and be righteous, but it is not our own righteousness we are to manifest; it is the righteousness of Jesus in our lives. In our relationship with Jesus we connect to the heart of our Father.

As a mother I do believe that I innately want to connect my family, especially my children, to other people and healthy community. I want them to be accepted and valued in certain social circles; circles that will benefit their future. First, it is essential to teach my children how to connect to the heart of our Father, our Creator, through a relationship with Jesus.

Continuing in Matthew 6:33, we read that if we seek His Kingdom and righteousness first, "all these things will be given to you also." This begs the questions, "What things?" I believe the answer to this question is found earlier in the same chapter.

"No one can serve two masters; for either he will hate the one and
love the other, or he will be devoted to the one and despise the
other. You cannot serve God and mammon [money, possessions,
fame, status, or whatever is valued more than the Lord]."
Matthew 6:24 (AMP)

The second part of this verse reveals the things the human heart
stresses over and has anxiety about, and this is amplified when we
have children. We want the best for our children; this is natural. As a
result, we can easily find ourselves stressing over finances, material
things (such as clothes, food, toys, yards, vehicles), status in the
community, education, health, houses, friends. The list is long. We
want to connect our children, our family, to the very best of each of
these things on our list.

To do that we must be obedient to the order of Scripture. First
connect ourselves, then lead and teach our children to connect to the
heart of the Father, seeking His Kingdom and righteousness first.
Then, all these things that weigh our hearts down will be taken care
of as a byproduct of keeping the order. These byproducts may not
come in the timing or packaging our hearts desire, but if we are truly
in line with the Word of God we can trust that God's way is best.
Remember, our God created and designed us to be in a relationship
with Him. There is no need to be tired and stressed. Follow the script
of God's Word. Order is everything.

As I reflect on my relationship with my mother as a child this
revelation about order shifted my perspective. I can see my mother
was robbed of being the connector in our family by the spirit of
religion. She did her best with what she knew. She was never taught
how to connect to the heart of the Father herself and therefore didn't
know how to teach us how to either. The stress, frustration and
tension in my childhood home was due to not following the order of
connecting as laid out in our script, the Bible.

By the grace of God this spirit of religion gets cut off from this family with me. This spirit does not have to be passed down to my children. We can burn this box, along with the last one, and educate ourselves on what the Word of God says about who we are, how we are to look to others and the order in which we connect. We also must be prepared to rebuke this spirit as it tries to re-enter our heart, because I know it will try.

Remain Teachable

My goal is to be completely free and confident in who I was made to be and to be filled with abundant joy that cannot be shaken by people or circumstances. If I want the results I am seeking all the ingredients must be in the right order.

Making yummy desserts is something I love to do, especially Nanaimo bars. If you have never heard of a Nanaimo bar, look it up. It is a delicious three-layered dessert bar consisting of a graham cracker crumb base and a creamy custard center topped with a smooth chocolate ganache. YUM! To make them successfully you not only need all the right ingredients, you must also add each ingredient in a particular order. I remember one time when I ignored the order of the ingredients and put the egg and the butter into the bowl at the same time. I soon learned how important it is to add each ingredient in a particular order to get the desired result.

Further, in this three-layered dessert it is essential for the layers to be in a set sequence or else the dessert bar will be a complete flop. Imagine putting the creamy custard as the base layer and the graham crumb solid as the center? This dessert bar would be a sloppy mess as it got removed from the pan. Rather than eating the bar with your hand it would need to be eaten with a spoon. In a similar way there are key ingredients and an order needed for your healing and preparation before you enter your abundant life in the Kingdom.

Neither freedom or abundant joy can be forced. Do not speed through positioning your heart. If you are not getting the results you desire take the time to examine every ingredient. Have you recognized and acknowledge the lies in your life? Have you forgiven those who hurt you? Have you repented for elevating your way above God's? Have you taken personal responsibility for your healing? Have you searched your heart with God to clean out your long-term storage? Are you continually choosing to draw close to the Father and purposefully deepen your relationship with Him?

Do not plow through this. In order to be activated in the Kingdom in the field you were designed for you must have a healed heart. Make sure all the ingredients are there and in order. Truly it comes down to your commitment. How committed are you to your own healing? God has promised to set you and me free. He is so committed to our freedom and healing He sent His one and only Son, Jesus, down to earth to live a sin-free life. He was so committed to His purpose on earth, Jesus *never* gave into a single temptation even when He was starving in the desert. He never gave up when He was being beaten to a pulp for crimes He *never* committed. He *never* gave up on us! Jesus being the model we are to follow should encourage us to *never* give up on ourselves.

Stay committed to your healing especially when it is the toughest and you feel like you are starving in the desert, being asked to give up your purpose for a slice of bread. That is when it matters the most. God has promised your freedom, and He is not slow in keeping His promises. He is just being extremely patient with us in our preparation. He is patient as we get our ingredients together and in the right order.

Esther was a bride who made herself ready. She did one year of preparation before her name was called and she stepped into the role she was made for. If you are not familiar with the story of Esther here is a brief summary. Queen Vashti failed to conduct herself in a pleasing way to the King Ahasuerus, and as a result lost her position as queen. As time goes on the king grows miserable. Nothing makes him happy. In an attempt to help, the king's advisors suggest a beauty pageant of sorts as a way to find a new queen. The king agrees, and many young ladies, including Esther, were gathered from the community. It is important to note that each woman chosen to participate in this beauty pageant was essentially given an invitation to stand before a king.

Even though they each had an invitation, they could not stand before Him until they had completed a year's worth of beauty treatments and royal etiquette training.

"Now when it was each young woman's turn to go before King Ahasuerus, after the end of her twelve months under the regulations for the women—for the days of their beautification were completed as follows: six months with oil of myrrh and six months with [sweet] spices *and* perfumes and the beauty preparations for women— then the young woman would go before the king in this way: anything that she wanted was given her to take with her from the harem into the king's palace. In the evening she would go in and the next morning she would return to the second harem, to the custody of Shaashgaz, the king's eunuch who was in charge of the concubines. She would not return to the king unless he delighted in her and she was summoned by name.
Now *as for* Esther, the daughter of Abihail the uncle of Mordecai who had taken her in as his [own] daughter, when her turn came to go in to the king, she requested nothing except what Hegai the king's eunuch [and attendant] who was in charge of the women, advised. And Esther found favor in the sight of all who saw her."
Esther 2:12-15 (AMP)

Preparation to stand before royalty is not unusual. Even if you were to go and meet Queen Elizabeth today you would be instructed on the proper manner in which to conduct yourself in her presence. However, in Esther's story these women had a full 12 months of preparation. There was no coming straight off the street and stepping into the position of a queen. No! It required a whole year in preparation just to stand before the king with the hope he would be pleased with you.

Like Esther, we are a bride being prepared to meet our King, King Jesus. We have the invitation, and if you have received Jesus as your personal Lord and Savior you have accepted that invitation. If you haven't, the invitation is waiting for you to accept. Do it today, don't wait.

Since accepting His invitation we've entered a time of preparation, getting ready to meet our King. Unlike Esther, our preparation will be for the rest of our lives, being washed and scrubbed of the dirt collected from the harsh elements of our daily lives. Sin has made us dirty. Many times the dirt isn't our fault (hence all the heart cleaning we just did). The devil uses others to make us dirty so that we are not King worthy.

The good news is that we are cleansed by the work Jesus did on the cross. When we accepted Jesus' invitation to be his bride all our sin was nailed to the cross, and we will stand before our King as a spotless beautiful bride. Even though all our sins are forgiven, dirt, wounds and junk from our past stick, preventing us from connecting with the heart of the Father and entering our full purpose while here on earth.

The devil loves playing the part of the accuser, reminding us that we will never be worthy enough to be the bride of a King, but that is simply not true. We *are* worthy because He says we are. He is the one who has chosen us to be His bride.

King Ahasuerus was pleased with Esther and called her by name to come into His presence as his bride. Like Esther, our King will call us by name to come into His presence and be His bride.

"Husbands, love your wives [seek the highest good for her and surround her with a caring, unselfish love], just as Christ also loved the church and gave Himself up for her, so that He might sanctify the church, having cleansed her by the washing of water with the word [of God], so that [in turn] He might present the church to Himself in glorious splendor, without spot or wrinkle or any such thing; but that she would be holy [set apart for God] and blameless." Ephesians 5:25-27 (AMP)

Esther had specific ingredients, such as oil of myrrh, spices and perfumes, for her preparation as well as overseers, teachers and trainers guiding her through the process. Without the aid of experienced teachers showing her what to do and when to do it Esther may never have been properly prepared for her meeting with the king. She needed to submit herself to the expertise of others and trust their insight. Even when it was her turn to go before the king Esther "requested nothing except what Hegai the king's eunuch [and attendant] who was in charge of the women, advised" (Esther 2:15 AMP).

What we need to pay attention to here is that Esther did not pretend to know what was best nor did she declare herself ready. We are never to think that we don't need help or wise counsel. It is dangerous to assume we know how to wash ourselves from the years of abuse and mistreatment or think we know the best strategies for our healing. We did not make ourselves, and we do not know ourselves like our Creator does. He sees the heart. He knows what we need and when we need it. With this in mind it is essential that we remain teachable.

Being teachable means having a good attitude to listen to the wisdom from God-fearing people, learning from them and applying what you learn. As we submit to the Lord and commit ourselves to our healing He will give us the ingredients we need and provide strategies. The Lord will use God-fearing people to show us the order. We must remain teachable, especially when it is uncomfortable or feels offensive. I am sure many of Esther's treatments were terribly uncomfortable or maybe even embarrassing. Who knows how invasive and personal those aiding her in the cleansing were? Be warned: it may feel like some people get too invasive or too personal with you. Choose *not* to be offended so you don't risk delaying your healing.

Remember the order. Intentionally seek to connect with the heart of your Father and He will connect you to the right people you need for your healing. Being teachable is a key ingredient for posturing our hearts to be who we were designed to be.

Search My Heart, Oh God!

I have now unboxed and trashed six dusty boxes found in the storage places of my heart. There may be more, so please do not think these are an exhaustive list of junk or stronghold spirits that could be found in hearts. These are the boxes the Lord has recently led me to clean out of my heart, and these were the revelations He gave me at this time. Going through them can position my heart to be used by Him in the way He wants at this time in my life. And please don't think this is all I have to deal with either. God is not done with me yet! In His time and in His way He will reveal to me more boxes I still don't realize are there.

In my experience cleaning not only takes time, it is also continuous. We don't just shower once and call ourselves clean for the rest of our lives. That would be disgusting! In the same way we must continue to return to the Father, asking Him to search our hearts to see if anything has snuck in that doesn't belong. When the Lord reveals ungodly attitudes or characteristics in us we must immediately allow the Lord to lead us through a cleaning. This journey has taught me to not waste time in getting it done. If it doesn't get done when the Lord reveals it, it has the potential to grow into a bigger mess, and bigger messes are harder and more time consuming to clean up.

Be obedient to the Word of God and deal with every box when the Lord reveals it to you. Also know God sometimes waits to reveal a box to us because He loves us and will not give us more than we can handle at a time (1 Cor. 10:13).

How Do I Search My Heart And Pitch The Boxes?

Now let's ask God to search our hearts and reveal the harmful junk, the spiritual strongholds, hiding in our hearts. Other boxes you may find in your heart's storage places could include Rebellion, Bitterness, Anger, Envy, Discourse, Worthlessness, Perfection, Flattery, Perversion, etc. You may be tempted to either rush through the process or to ignore or delay it. I encourage you to give it the proper time and attention. Stay committed and keep your eyes on the goal: freedom and an abundantly joy-filled life.

You might be thinking *how do I pitch the boxes I find?* I choose to use prayer to get rid of the unwanted boxes in my heart and close the door of access to enemy to prevent them from returning. I do this through repentance, forgiveness and renouncing lies I have believed and partnered with. I give these things to Jesus and ask Him to replace what I give Him with whatever He chooses.

A great place to begin is by asking God questions, then wait for an answer. For me the answer often pops into my head either as words or pictures. Pictures can be pictures of a memory. I know it is from God because it often surprises me with its accuracy and it is most often something I wasn't thinking about or had totally forgotten about. When praying and asking God these questions you do not have to use the name "God." You may use whatever name of God connects you to His heart. You may want to use Daddy, Abba, Papa God, Father, Heavenly Father, or Holy Spirit.

Ask: "Heavenly Father, is there a lie I am believing about You or myself?"

Did anything come to your mind? Words, pictures, memories? If so, write down.

Ask: "Papa God, where did this lie come from?"

Write down what God reveals to you. If the Lord reveals a person to you, such as your mother, choose to forgive that person now. Forgiving them is releasing yourself from them in this specific area.

Pray: "Father, I choose to forgive _____ (person) for giving the enemy an access point into my heart and placing the box of _____ there. I repent for believing this lie and for any and every way I partnered with this lie and allowed it to influence my thinking and actions. Father, I choose to give this lie to You, this horrible box from my heart. Take it away from me. Father, reveal to me now the truth."

Write down what He tells you.

Pray: "In exchange for this lie/box, what do You give me?"

Wait a moment in silence for His answer. When you have the answer, thank Him.

Pray: "Father, thank you for giving me _____ (joy, peace, compassion, love, etc.)."

Praise the Lord! When I have these exchanges with my Heavenly Father I feel so light and closer to Him. I love that feeling. At this time I like to put on some worship music and just praise Him. God is so good!

Unboxed Prayer

Dear Father,

Thank you for exposing all the junk-filled boxes in my heart and for providing a way for me to get rid of them forever. Thank you for chasing after me, choosing me and fighting for my freedom and wholeness. Thank you for not abandoning Your purpose for me but guiding me to fulfill it. I am following You wherever You lead. Fill me with Your Holy Spirit. Consume me with Your fire and seal all the work You have done in me with the blood of Your Son, Yeshua, so Your name may be glorified with my life.

· SEVEN ·

Obedience, My Love Choice

Many years ago I had a very vivid dream that I still think about from time to time. I believe this dream was a warning; a warning I didn't listen to soon enough. In this dream I was in the church I grew up in. My mother was there along with many other people. It was cleaning day, and many people from the congregation were there helping. The only person I remember recognizing was my mother. While sweeping the floor my mother was across the room cleaning something else. When I finished sweeping there was a nice little pile of dirt. I did not have a dust pan so I asked my mom where I could find one.

My mother said, "You don't need one; we just sweep it under the rug." Very surprised, I questioned her answer, and my mother informed me there was a hole under the rug so "Just sweep the dirt in the hole." I picked up the rug with one hand and sure enough, there was a hole about the size of a dinner plate. I remember feeling like *this is so wrong, sweeping this dirt under the rug.*

It was the church I grew up in, but I no longer attended since moving away to college. I didn't consider it my church any more, but I was just there to help while visiting my parents. As a visitor helper, I did what I was told and began to sweep the dirt into the hole under the rug.

As I swept the edges of the hole were caving in, making the hole bigger and bigger. Surprised and a little scared I started to back up while staring at this hole in complete disbelief. I didn't back up fast enough. The speed of the caving edges was accelerating, and before I recognized what was happening the floor underneath my feet collapsed into the hole. I was terrified, frantically grasping for anything to keep me from falling in. At the same time I was screaming for help.

The disturbing thing was no one in that church moved. No one saw the floor caving in. No one heard my screams. No one came to help. No one, including my mother who was standing right there. Everyone continued with their tasks as if nothing was wrong. I lost the battle, and as I fell in I woke up from this nightmare.

Eager to find out the meaning of the dream I shared it with a friend who I knew hears from the Lord and is filled with the Holy Spirit. She directed me to a book by Ira Milligan. She also said she strongly felt whatever church or group of people that dream represented I needed to get out of. I remember thinking the dream was truly referring to the church I grew up in and my mother. That church, my mother and her church friends were toxic to my emotional health. Not being completely certain of the dream's interpretation I became cautious with churches we attended from then on just in case it was a warning dream of a future congregation I may get involved with.

However, as I have reflected on that dream the past 12 years of my life I believe this dream (along with the counsel I received and what I have experienced) was a true warning concerning my mother and the system of values I was raised in. There are so many holes in my own story that may never get filled. This dream at least gives me an understanding of spiritual atmosphere of my childhood. It was toxic. The dream confirms what I sensed about hidden things in my family's history. I may never know all the things that have been swept under the rug, and I am fine with that. God knows. Furthermore, this affirms my mother genuinely does not see my suffering. I could be screaming for my life, and she carries on as if I am not even there.

This does not create anger in me, rather compassion. She must be hurting deeply herself to be blinded to the pain of her own daughter. I pray my mother finds the boldness to not ignore her own heart wounds and begin taking the steps she needs to with the Lord to begin her own healing journey.

Finally, from this dream I learned to pay attention to the warnings. Be more diligent and attentive in praying over dreams and listening to the direction of the Father. I learned to not hesitate in being obedient to the Lord especially when it is the most difficult. My ways are not better than God's. He knows what is best because He sees the bigger picture. My ways tried to address what I could see and feel in the flesh. God's ways address what is happening in the spiritual realm; the realm I cannot see but greatly affects the physical realm. The reason God's ways are higher and better than ours is that our fight is not against the flesh.

"For our struggle is not against flesh and blood, but against the rulers, against the authorities, against the powers of this dark world and against the spiritual forces of evil in the heavenly realms."
Ephesians 6:12 (NIV)

What Is Obedience?

The KingJamesBibleDictionary.com defines obedience as "Compliance with a command, prohibition or known law and rule of duty prescribed; the performance of what is required or enjoined by authority, or the abstaining from what is prohibited, in compliance with the command or prohibition. To constitute OBEDIENCE the act or forbearance to act must be in submission to authority; the command must be known to the person, and his compliance must be in consequence of it, or it is not OBEDIENCE. OBEDIENCE is not synonymous with obsequiousness; the latter often implying meanness or servility, and OBEDIENCE being merely a proper submission to authority. That which duty requires implies dignity of conduct rather than servility. OBEDIENCE may be voluntary or involuntary. Voluntary OBEDIENCE alone can be acceptable to God."

To summarize, obedience is a choice to comply with a command, rule or law required by an authority. As a citizen of the Kingdom of Heaven the law or "code of conduct" (as I like to say) is the Word of God, the Bible, and the authority we choose to submit to is Yahweh God, the King of Kings, and His Son Jesus, the Living Word. Obedience to God is not done out of fear, an effort to gain favor or to make ourselves "good." If you obey God because you are afraid of Him you don't really know God. If you are obeying God to gain favor, then you are missing the point. If you define how good of a person you are by how well you obey you are not living the life you are called to.

None of these kinds of obedience is what our God wants. We do not have to earn points with our God in an effort to be "good enough" for Him. In my past obedience was often done either out of fear of the consequences or because I was trying to be "good enough" to earn love and affection from my mother.

Being obedient is not what qualifies us to be worthy of love. Love is not earned. We do not have to earn God's love. He loves you because you are you. We didn't have to do anything for His love. It is there for us. We just need to accept it. Obedience is loving Him back. This is pure love, pure freedom and a full life.

This is hard to wrap our minds around especially coming out of abusive relationships where love was so conditional. Our need to feel good enough or adequate, whether conscious or unconscious, is deeply rooted in our relationship with our mothers. In my relationship with my mother I always felt if I was good enough I would feel loved by her. Unfortunately that did not happen in my numerous attempts. She was unable to offer unconditional love to me. This helps me understand why the two of us never really bonded; we had "attachment" issues, as they would say in psychology.

As a result, the lie that *love must be earned by being good* has messed with my mindsets, shaped my thinking and has messed with my heart, which forms the core of who I am. If it hasn't already been established clearly let me say it again: as we accept God's unconditional love His love fills the storage places of our hearts. Then, the love in our hearts will come out of our mouths, and the world around us will know love is at the core of our beings. Love that was never earned. Love with no strings attached. Love without conditions. Love that reflects the Father and draws others closer to Him. Love which releases our true selves unapologetically. Love that demonstrates confidence in who we were created to be.

Obedience Is Better Than Sacrifice

I can't talk about obedience without at least mentioning this scripture:

"But Samuel replied:
'Does the Lord delight in burnt offerings and sacrifices
as much as in obeying the Lord?
To obey is better than sacrifice,
and to heed is better than the fat of rams.'"
1 Samuel 15:22 (AMP)

Let's highlight, "To obey is better than sacrifice." If you are not familiar with the history behind this verse here is a quick overview. Samuel, a prophet, went to Saul, the King of Israel, with this message from the Lord: "Now go, attack the Amalekites and totally destroy all that belongs to them. Do not spare them; put to death men and women, children and infants, cattle and sheep, camels and donkeys" (1 Samuel 15:3 AMP). Unfortunately Saul decided to keep the Amalekite king alive and take the plunder rather than destroy it. Saul had clearly disobeyed the instruction of the Lord. Samuel confronted Saul about his disobedience. Saul did admit what he did was wrong, but the deed was already done and the consequences were unavoidable. He lost God's anointing as King over Israel.

"Samuel said to him, 'The Lord has torn the kingdom of Israel from you today and has given it to one of your neighbors—to one better than you.'" 1 Samuel 15:28 (AMP)

Saul's disobedience was rebellious, sinful, idolatrous and disrespectful to the word of God spoken through the prophet. Consequently Saul lost not only his position but later his life. Saul's excuse for his disobedience was, "I was afraid of the men and so I gave in to them" (1 Sam. 15:24). Still today God's people place too much value in looking good to those around them – friends, peers, community, co-workers – and sacrifice God's blessings for temporary comfort and acceptance from people (who probably don't care about them at all anyway). These people are not going to be lying awake at night thinking about how good we look to them. So why do we continue to value the opinions of others over obeying the Word of the Lord?

I can relate to Saul; fear of man has kept me from obeying more times than I care to admit. This includes the writing of this book. It has taken me more than ten years to obey the Lord in this. I feared I wasn't a "good enough" writer, no one would want to read it and mostly that no one would believe my story was traumatic enough to be noticed. It wasn't until the Lord got a hold of me and said *it doesn't matter what anyone else thinks of this book.* It doesn't matter if anyone reads it at all. The point is He told me to write it, and His request needs to be enough for me to obey. I also need to trust...if God has said it is good, then there is a blessing in it.

The only reasons we would disobey the Lord would be rebellion, idolatry, disrespect and fear of man which are all sin. Jesus died on the cross for all of our sins so we can have life and have it to the fullest. So why would we sacrifice an abundant life to protect emotions that are not eternal?

With disobedience comes a heaviness you can't shake off. You carry it wherever you go. It weighs you down and has you longing for freedom. It is hard to explain to others who are not believers and who do not understand, but there is a true heaviness that accompanies disobedience. This weight can only be lifted through the act of true love and obeying our Heavenly Father. He is a good Father and would not ask you to do something if it wasn't good or didn't have a blessing attached to it. I know I am trusting in that with writing this book. I am learning to love, to truly love and trust my Savior by allowing myself to be a vessel to write the story He chooses. I am His and my life is part of an even greater story I can't image.

Although our mothers were used as unsuccessful vessels to destroy from the inside out the twist in the plot is you and I have become vessels for the Lord to use for good. We are now vessels used for healing and restoration from the inside out. Do not sacrifice your opportunity to be a beautiful vessel in the greatest story ever written. As a Kingdom of Heaven citizen make the conscious decision to love deeply in your obedience to the Word of the Lord. Obedience is your love choice.

Why Is Obedience So Necessary?

Our choice to obey God is out of love – our love for Him because He first loved us. When we truly love God nothing comes before Him. This is not to say we are obligated to fulfill a list of His demands, and if we don't we are deemed unworthy. No! Living in a way feeling like you have to fulfill someone else's demands while suffering emotionally, mentally and spiritually is bondage and the complete opposite of how God wants us to live. Remember, Jesus also said, "I came that they may have and enjoy life, and have it in abundance [to the full, till it overflows]" (John 10:10). Love is freeing, not bondage.

When we equate obeying God to loving God it can sound so simple. What do we do for people we love? We spend time with them, we listen to them, we don't do things that will hurt them. We are open with them, we honor them, we share in their joys and in their pain. We are there for them. These actions create the potential for a beautiful and perfect relationship. However, as simple as it sounds the reality is we live in a fallen world. The distractions in our everyday lives can be overwhelming, and our relationship with God can almost be forgotten. Our pain from the wounds of an emotionally abusive mother is a distraction preventing us from loving God over and above our pain. Growing up with an abusive parent can give us a distorted idea of what love really is. Learning what real love is and how to love is learning how to obey God, because loving Him is obeying Him, and in obeying Him we find our true self.

"The [intrinsically] good man produces what is good *and* honorable *and* moral out of the good treasure [stored] in his heart; and the [intrinsically] evil *man* produces what is wicked *and* depraved out of the evil [in his heart]; for his mouth speaks from the overflow of his heart." Luke 6:45 (AMP)

I love this verse because it reminds me how obedience to the Lord will fill the core of who I am with "good treasure," the kind I was designed to have in the first place. The good treasure is my true self. Living to meet someone else's standard of good enough is not the real me and it is not the real you. This pursuit also makes us feel miserably stuck. Real love doesn't make you feel like you are constantly falling short. You have not fallen short, you are not a failure, you are not worthless and you are deserving of love because God, your Creator, says so. His standard is the only standard that matters. He is good, and as a citizen of Heaven His Spirit resides in you. Therefore, you are good. The standard is set; let no person destroy that.

"The second is like it, 'You shall love your neighbor as yourself [that is, unselfishly seek the best or higher good for others].' The whole Law and the [writings of the] Prophets depend on these two commandments." Matthew 22:39-40 (AMP)

If your heart is so full of God's love and His treasures loving your neighbor will be natural; it will be the natural overflow of your heart (Luke 6:45). I believe *neighbor* may be interpreted as being whoever you happen to be near in every situation. It could be your family, your friends or your literal neighbors. It could also be the people standing in line with you at the grocery store, your co-workers, your children's teachers and your mother.

Even though the root of needing to feel "good enough" through obedience came from my mother there can be different reasons leading to this exhausting behavior. For me, I believe there was a hidden belief that I could control my surroundings. My mother was manipulative. Remember the story I shared earlier in this book about how my mother taught me to not hit other children? The time I followed what I was taught and restrained myself from hitting the little girl who hit my sister I felt punished rather than the anticipated praise. So proud of myself for obeying, I felt I had finally earned the good enough place in her heart. Maybe even a pat on the head with an "I am proud of you! You did the right thing." These kinds of instances were laced throughout my life; times when I thought I made it in the door, only to be crushed as she slammed it hard in my face.

The Lord has revealed to me a hidden habit that formed: I had to control my surroundings through manipulative tactics I learned at a young age from my mother. In my attempts to be good enough I was manipulating. I had no idea I was even doing it. Manipulation is one of my mother's characteristics I hated so much, yet I came to realize I had been doing it myself. Reflecting on this revelation, the Lord continues to reveal this truth to me, and I will admit it is a little overwhelming.

Ironically I wasn't even allowing *myself* to be good enough. I was critical and judgmental of myself. Again I find myself on my knees in a place of repentance. I recognize I cannot be filled with His love and obey His Word through loving Him if I continue operating in this behavior and thinking, using manipulative strategies to control my surroundings. I can't.

151

My self-esteem has been more damaged in my childhood than I had originally thought. Even so I am confident there is nothing our God cannot heal and restore. Obedience is necessary because it leads us away from sin and fleshly behavior, resulting in living out our true self the way we were designed to.

Commit To The Name Of Yeshua

When you are in a loving relationship with a special someone you are committed to that person. Loving someone means you commit to being loyal and faithful to them. It is no different with your relationship with Jesus. Obeying Jesus is loving Him and being committed to His name and what He stands for. Commitment to the name of Jesus goes deeper than your initial declaration of Him being Lord of your life and believing in your heart God raised Him from the dead (Romans 10:9). Yes, you are saved if you have done so, but your obedience to Him is a continual act of commitment.

Remember, as a Kingdom of Heaven citizen obedience means we have made the conscious decision to obey the Word of God. In that decision we commit to the name of Jesus, for Jesus is the Living Word (John 1). Therefore, we must let the Word speak for itself, not adding to it or taking away from it (Deut. 4:2, Deut. 12:32, Rev. 22:18).

Committing ourselves to the name of Jesus is a choice. In this choice we are committing to study the Word for what it actually says, not what we perceive it to say or what others have told us it says. Knowing the Word of God equips us to discern when the Word is being misused. People may try to manipulate a situation to control the outcome according to their own desires and not God's. In my life people have used the Word of God to manipulate or control me. As I step out from under the control of my abusive mother I need to understand the Word for myself so it can't be used against me to make me feel guilty or shameful for decisions I choose to make. May my actions and words never cause confusion about who God is, who I am in Him and who I am committed to.

As I began writing this section of my book I listened to an anointed teaching by Jason Porter titled *Christmust*. This teaching seemed to fit this topic of committing to the name of Jesus so well. Even though the particular point of Porter's message is not the exact point I am making here, God used the scriptures in it to highlight the depth and strength of our commitment. I genuinely love when God works like this. When God is highlighting something to me everywhere I go He speaks to me about it.

God's Word is here to wash us and clean us. It will sometimes hurt or be incredibly uncomfortable, but God calls us to obey His Word. It's not because He is a mean God on a power trip, wanting to control us with an iron fist. If that were the case He would not create us with a free will to choose Him, to choose to love Him, to choose to follow Him, to choose to believe in His Son. Jesus came to establish a Kingdom here on earth that we are invited to be a part of. This Kingdom is not dirty and requires those who enter to be washed by the Word.

"The Son of Man will send out His angels, and they will gather out of His kingdom all things that offend [those things by which people are led into sin], and all who practice evil [leading others into sin]."
Matthew 13:41 (AMP)

The angels are coming to gather things that offend God's Kingdom. Angels are special messengers sent by God. This is why sometimes you will see angels referred to as messengers. In Revelation 2 we read a letter written to the angel of the church of Ephesus. Pastor Jason Porter points out "Yeshua's messengers, angels, are sent to accurately report and transmit His message and remove anything and anyone who removes or distorts it."

Seriously, this is heavy. We must submit to His Word washing us NOW or else it will be done for us later. I understand getting washed, rebuked and corrected is not fun. I personally don't like it. I will often try to avoid it. The truth is each of us will be judged by God. Before that time it is our choice to obey God's Word and allow Scripture to correct our mindsets and in turn our behaviors.

Even if it hurts and is uncomfortable or possibly embarrassing we need to know, if God says it, it is ultimately there to bless us and glorify Him. Honestly we should be thanking God for His Word; without it we wouldn't know what to do and would be left wondering or guessing if what we are doing is *good enough*. There it is again...*good enough*.

When the Word of God corrects us there is no need to become offended. I have been getting checked by God's Word throughout this whole book-writing process. I deeply believe the Word of the Lord for me was to finish this book before the new year. Why? I do not exactly know. However, I trust there is blessing in the obedience. Fear and feelings of inadequacy may have stopped me for a while but at the core of the issue was disobedience. Yet in this season I have such an inner sense of urgency to complete this, and I have to trust it is for something greater than myself – to advance the Kingdom in whatever way He chooses. So, here I am, walking out what God has called me to do (1 Cor. 7:17, Rev. 3:11).

In 2 Kings we read about king after king, what they did wrong, what they did right, then more of what they did wrong. It can feel almost tedious and boring reading about each king, but with careful study of the text we are able see past the long list of kings and find some gold nuggets relatable to our present lives.

Taking a closer look we see the list doesn't just stop with who did what was right or wrong. Even if they were a good king there was another level of dedication God paid attention to: whether or not they kept the "high places." It wasn't *good enough* to just be a good king. See, the good enough comes back around again as we dive deeper into Scripture, reminding us that our own efforts outside of God will always fall short of earning the "good enough" badge. The devil's strategies to keep God's people from fulfilling their purpose have not changed from ancient times. Why change the strategy if it works so well?

154

In his teaching, Pastor Jason Porter made this statement: "You can be saved, filled with the Holy Spirit, Jesus will love you, Jesus will bless you, but He will still have a problem with the high places, or the compromises in your life." Ouch! To reach the high level of commitment and intimacy with Jesus needed to fulfill our prophetic calling in the Kingdom it is necessary to deal with every high place in our lives. I am talking about the high places we have set up ourselves and not what our mother put on us.

What have we chosen to tolerate that stands in the way of our complete freedom? It is no longer an excuse to blame our actions and thinking patterns on our abusive mother, no matter how emotionally painful it has been. Again we revisit the significance of personal responsibility. We are in charge our ourselves. God has given each of us our own domain to rule; how we rule is our choice. We cannot blame our mother.

Now let's go back to the list of kings. In 1 and 2 Kings only two kings chose to get rid of the high places – Josiah and Hezekiah. These high places were shrines, alters and poles put up to honor the gods Baal and Ashtoreth. Hezekiah is a king we can all relate to, please pay attention.

King Hezekiah loved the Lord, he trusted the Lord, he was faithful to the Lord and obeyed His commandments (2 Kings 18:5-6). In King Hezekiah's story he seems to experience regret and doubt after obeying the Lord because his enemy attacks. I can relate to King's Hezekiah's mixed emotions after obeying God. After finally obeying God by stepping away from my mother and establishing a firm boundary I remember a series of unfortunate events occurred one after the other for months. I found myself asking, "Did I make the right decision?" In my heart I knew I had and stayed committed to the firm boundary despite each attack.

I actually never made the connection between all these unfortunate events and my boundary decision until after weeks of sharing with a fellow church volunteer all the crazy things going on in my life. One Sunday he finally asked, "Did you recently take a strong stand spiritually?" That question immediately connected all the dots. I was being attacked for being obedient to the Lord and taking this strong stand. It wasn't because I made the wrong decision.

In 2 Kings 18 King Hezekiah made the right choice too by obeying the word of the Lord and removing all the shrines, smashing the altars and elements used in pagan worship and cutting down the Asherah poles. King Hezekiah experienced success and the Lord's blessings in his obedience. His confidence was so great in the Lord that he revolted against and refuse to pay tribute to the King of Assyria (2 Kings 18:7). However, this confidence wavered in the years to come.

Years after King Hezekiah took the throne he heard of the Assyrian King conquering the northern part of Israel, and then later all the fortified cities of Judah. The Assyrian king only needed to take Jerusalem to completely conquer Judah. King Hezekiah, seeing how God had not intervened in the capture of all these other cities, had a giant moment of doubt. Would God intervene and save Jerusalem? As a result, he took it upon himself to make a decision he felt was wise in the moment: becoming a subject of the Assyrian king instead of trusting God to save Jerusalem. To save his city King Hezekiah proceeded to give the king of Assyria anything he wanted, including stripping the temple of its gold and silver.

Later the king of Assyria sent messengers with an army to deliver a significant message.

"Then the Rabshakeh said to them, 'Say to Hezekiah,
'Thus says the great king, the king of Assyria, "What is [the reason for] this confidence that you have?"'" 2 Kings 18:19 (AMP)

Do you see it? The Assyrians were confused. The Assyrians knew King Hezekiah worshiped Yahweh, and they further knew he removed the high places used for worship. They initially saw King Hezekiah's confidence to revolt against and refuse to pay tribute to the king of Assyria, yet now his confidence seemed to quickly melt away. The Assyrians saw King Hezekiah completely compromise his faith in a moment of doubt. But the enemies incorrectly interpreted his compromise; they confused the high places with Yahweh.

"But perhaps you will say to me, 'We are trusting in the Lord our God!' But isn't he the one who was insulted by Hezekiah? Didn't Hezekiah tear down his shrines and altars and make everyone in Judah and Jerusalem worship only at the altar here in Jerusalem?"
2 Kings 18:22 (NLT)

King Hezekiah feared, then doubted. The enemy may have seen this as King Hezekiah making a terrible mistake by offending his God (by tearing down his God's altars), and now he is scared of the consequences. They thought he had nothing to put his confidence in. The high places were not Yahweh's; they never were. Yet Hezekiah's actions still did not represent his God, and the enemy had no idea who his God actually was. Don't miss the significance of this.

We see a similar thing happen Exodus 32. Here the Israelites were just led out of Egypt by the miraculous hand of God, and we read they are constructing a golden calf to worship. Wait, what? How could they, right? We have all read this passage and thought the Israelites were idiots for so quickly forgetting their miraculous deliverance from slavery. Can you relate? I know I can.

Let's be honest, God moves in our lives in a big way, answers a desperate prayer, provides in a supernatural way or opens a long-awaited door of some kind. We are so touched and moved we think we would never doubt God again, but then we do. Oops!

"Then Aaron took the gold, melted it down, and molded it into the shape of a calf. When the people saw it, they exclaimed, 'O Israel, these are the gods who brought you out of the land of Egypt!' Aaron saw how excited the people were, so he built an altar in front of the calf. Then he announced, 'Tomorrow will be a festival to the Lord!'" Exodus 32: 4-5 (NLT)

The Israelites make the calf and present it as the god who brought them out of Egypt. Then, we read Aaron made an altar before the calf and proclaimed, "Tomorrow will be a festival to the Lord." They literally just made an idol and slapped a God label on it...as if the God label made it all okay. It is amazing how people will take demonic things, pagan things, idolatrous things, and put the Lord's name on it. Putting a God label on these ungodly things have allowed people to justify their own actions and thoughts so they do not have to repent and change their ways. It is a crutch and a way of avoiding pain. And yes, this has happened and is happening abundantly in this day and age.

The devil's strategy to get God's people to compromise hasn't changed in literally thousands of years. When God's people take a firm stance with the Word of God, create a firm boundary with anything and anyone that does not align with God's Word, such as Hezikiah, or experience a supernatural breakthrough, like Aaron and the people of Israel, our enemy will come after us and attack us, either through people or events, in an attempt to have us doubt ourselves and compromise. From Aaron to Hezekiah we see this happening, and it still is today.

We are not being attacked because we made a wrong decision, we are being attacked because we made the *right* decision, the God decision. When we choose to put His Word first, we are taking power away from the enemy. The power the enemy had over us. In this way we are taking back our God given authority. One way the enemy attacked me in my relationship with my mother, is by confusing me on what the Word of God is and slapping the "God" label on actions that are actually abusive.

For example, when creating a boundary to protect myself from toxic, abusive behavior, I have been accused of being ungrateful and dishonoring. As a result, I doubted myself, thinking I am in the wrong. When I allow myself to agree that my boundary is wrong, it does not provoke any behavior change from my mother. This allows my mother to justify the behavior by misusing, twisting or misinterpreting the Word of God to avoid the discomfort and possible pain of repentance and change. Every time I have listened to this accusing voice from the enemy, forgot what God had said and went back on my decision for the sake of pleasing my mom, I have allowed a misrepresentation of my God, Jesus' name and have given some power back to the enemy to control me.

If God's people tolerate the misrepresentation of Jesus' name, it makes them guilty by association. This is why everything God deems bad, offensive, wrong or doesn't like should never be tolerated or compromised with. In our society people take things God clearly says are wrong in His Word and pressure God's people to tolerate it, and if you don't you are considered a "hater" and popular opinion says haters are not good followers of Christ. How did we get here? Tolerating things that are contrary to God's Word is not okay. Aaron wanted to please the people, so he did what they wanted him to do, even though he knew it was wrong. To justify his compromised action, he threw a "God" label on it. I wanted to please my mother, so I tried to do what she wanted me to do, I compromised what I knew to be true and slapped a "God" label on it as honoring my mother. This was a misrepresentation of my God and a false commitment to the name of Jesus. This was what is called being double-minded.

I had divided loyalties, and I needed to decide: was I committed to being who my mom wanted me to be, or was I committed to Jesus, His name and what He represents? When we commit ourselves to the name of Jesus we commit to being known for believing what Jesus believed. Let us make the stance and create the boundaries God is leading us to make. May we stand firm against every attack and weapon formed against us, and may we never forget what God has told us or what he has done for us.

When our abusive mother shows up, sends us texts, calls or reaches out to us in any way, do not fear. Don't even remember all the terrible, destructive and damaging things she has done to you in the past. Remember all the great things God has done for you in both the past and the present. King Hezekiah looked at the destruction of the enemy and feared; he didn't trust God or even give Him the opportunity to show Himself. This tore King Hezekiah's kingdom, his domain, apart. If we allow our mother to strike fear in us she could tear us down, bringing us back into bondage to her (ultimately to the devil who is using her as a vessel). And yes, I am writing from my personal experience.

We have been working at healing our hearts and renewing our minds, right? She may see the work you have done, and when you crumble in fear at the sound of her voice or see her name on the phone, she will be confused. Like with the enemies of King Hezekiah, the voice of the enemy will return: "You are pathetic. You are ridiculous. You say God is healing you. You say you have done all this work, for what? I do not see any difference in you at all. You have wasted your time. You have made no progress. You are exactly who you were before – nothing but an angry, selfish little girl." This stings a little writing this because this had been my story. But no more. Let's not be like King Hezekiah; let's stay committed.

"Hater!" Now that is a label that's been used a lot lately, both accurately and inaccurately. It has become a way of shaming others. If we choose to stay in our toxic relationship with our mothers out of fear of looking like a hater or a bad daughter, then we are choosing to live in a lie and misrepresent Jesus, which may confuse every non-believer around you. You are choosing to mix good with evil. That didn't turn out well in the garden of Eden, so why would it turn out well now? Just as a golden calf is not God, tolerating evil is NOT love. You are not a hater. You are lover of Jesus and His Word. Commit to the name of Jesus without the confusion.

The Ancient Way

"'Teacher, which is the greatest commandment in the Law?' And Jesus replied to him, 'You shall love the Lord your God with all your heart, and with all your soul, and with all your mind.' This is

the first and greatest commandment. The second is like it, 'You shall love your neighbor as yourself [that is, unselfishly seek the best or higher good for others].' The whole Law and the [writings of the] Prophets depend on these two commandments.'"
Matthew 22:36-40 (AMP)

In this scripture Jesus is clear about how, as Kingdom citizens, we are to obey. The first is to "love the Lord your God with all your heart, and with all your soul, and with all your mind." This isn't a new thought or idea Jesus is presenting to the people. He is actually quoting from the Old Testament.

"You shall love the Lord your God with all your heart *and* mind and with all your soul and with all your strength [your entire being]."
Deuteronomy 6:5 (AMP)

The steps to obedience have not changed from the beginning. God had Moses record it in the Torah (the first five books of the Bible), and Jesus quotes this more than a thousand years later declaring that the script hasn't changed. To obey God we must love Him with our entire being. This is also in line with the first of the Ten Commandments:

"You shall have no other gods before Me."
Exodus 20:3 (NIV)

Loving God with our obedience becomes easier and more natural the more we spend time with Him by studying His Word and communing with Him through prayer. I find asking God questions such as, "Why am I feeling this way?" "How do you feel about me?" "What do you have for me today?" draw me closer to my Heavenly Father. It strengthens our relationship and keeps me constantly practicing hearing His voice. This way obeying His Word is easier because the love relationship is established. I am more aware of His love for me and it is an honor to love Him back.

My Choice

Over the course of this book we have discovered, unpacked and navigated through several mindsets and thinking patterns that are rooted in our childhood. They have cluttered our mind and confused us on who God made us to be. If we don't know who we are, then how does any person, in any of our circles, know who we are? In our commitment to the name of Jesus we choose to allow the Holy Spirit to interpret the Word of God for us. In doing so the Word of God will clean out and declutter our minds from the filth of this fallen world. We want our Lord to deal with the things in us that are opposed to Him.

Being victims of emotional abuse, we have allowed our feelings to interpret the world around us rather than truth. This is dangerous because we can and have fallen victim to false narratives that have led us away from the very relationship we are created for – our relationship with our Creator Father. Let's choose now to put our feelings aside, not interpreting what we read through our emotions, but rather being attentive to what God is actually saying and what God wants us to know. The Word of God is not about making us feel better or about pointing out every one of our flaws. We see in the Bible the real Jesus is balanced. He gives us the good and the bad, and it is our choice what we choose to do with what He says.

Unboxed Prayer

Father in Heaven,

I love You so much and my heart is so full with Your love. May Your Word always be a lamp for my feet and light to my path. My heart's desire is to follow, walk and dance with You and Your Word all the days of my life. Meet me every day; may I always crave Your Word. May I demonstrate my love for You through my obedience.

Give me a heart for what You have a heart for. Give me Your eyes to see people the way You see them so I feel Your love for them in me.

In the mighty name of Jesus, AMEN!

EIGHT

Boundaries, My Right

My son is in tears. I hold him close, comforting his wounded heart. I feel sick to my stomach as guilt grows in my core, weakening my spirit and tempting me to shut down. Taking full responsibility for my son's pain, I felt it was my fault. I knew how powerfully manipulative my mother was and how crushing the weight of her tactics can be on the vulnerable. My son had broken under the pressure of his grandmother's forced desires. Tears begin swelling in my eyes as he shared how he felt he had to do what Grammie wanted or else she wouldn't stop pressuring him to do what he didn't want to. To please her he gave in, and was now dealing with the strong feelings of regret…the kind of regret no child should feel especially involving an adult they love and trust.

My mother was visiting for the week. The excitement of her arrival was dampened by her negative comments about my son's hair. She made it clear she didn't like it. He had been letting it grow out and it flowed in a skater like manner. He was really proud of his skater look, and honestly he rocked it. He looks great with longer hair, just like his daddy. However, long hair on men doesn't sit well with my mother.

We brushed off the first few negative jabs at the hair, but it was getting uncomfortable; she wouldn't let it go. Comments included, "Doesn't your mom cut your hair?" and "You would look so much more handsome with shorter hair." Soon my mother began to offer to pay for a haircut. My son declined. She asked, and he answered, and she should have stopped there, but she didn't. She offered to show him pictures of other boys with shorter hair, saying things like,

"You might see something you like, then I will take you to the salon and pay for your hair cut." My son repeatedly said no. My mom would not let up. A couple of times I intervened with, "Mom, he really likes his hair the way it is." My comments were either ignored or shot down with her opinion about boys and hair.

Mistakenly I chose to not step in any more than I did. *We can put up with this for a week, then she will be gone and we can go back to our hair-freedom living.* But I was too blind to see the impact it was having on my son and too naïve to believe my mother would push the issue too far.

One day my mother offered to take my son out to eat and do some shopping. I saw no harm in letting them spend time together, so I let them go. When they returned my son had short hair. I was shocked. "Mom, what happened?" She replied, "He agreed to it. I didn't do anything he didn't want to." Surprised, I pressed the issue a little stating, "But he loved his long hair. How did this happen?

My mother explained that she took him to the hair salon just to look at the books full of different hairstyles. She continued by saying, "He found a picture he liked, and since we were already there, we just went ahead and cut it to be like the picture. He agreed. I didn't do anything he didn't agree to." My mother went from constantly criticizing my son's hair to going out of her way to compliment it. She went over the top with her compliments to make it known how pleased she was with his short hair. My heart sunk, knowing he wasn't loving the new look. I didn't know what to do. It was like we took another lap around the merry-go-round.

Once again she pushed and manipulated until she got her way. My mother always seems so driven to have her way, obsessive even. Yet when I try to confront her, she backs up, becomes verbally and emotionally aggressive and takes no responsibility for any wounding her behavior causes. With my son, she took no responsibility for his wounded heart. My mother responded to my concern with, "If he doesn't like it, it isn't my fault. He agreed to it."

Holding my crying son, how do I explain to him that I completely understand how he feels? How do explain why I didn't protect him? Why did my son have to feel like Grammie didn't love him just the way he was, whatever length his hair? My mama heart was heavy seeing my son suffer the way I did from the same woman. I never in a million years would have thought my mother would treat my children the same way as she treated me. I was blinded from my own heart wounds and didn't see how she was negatively affecting my kids until I had a crying child in my arms.

"Jesus, where were You in this memory?" I ask my Lord. "Right there with you, holding My son."

The Holy Spirit shows me Jesus holding my son close to His chest, pouring His love and acceptance into his little body, mending his fragile heart right there. A beautiful sense of peace sweeps over me, and I knew everything was going to be okay. I knew my son's heart was not going to be wounded the way mine was. I knew healing was happening in this moment; my son would not be blinded by heart wounds the way I was.

Boundaries Introduced

This situation with my son, I believe, would have been prevented if I had taken the counsel of many God-fearing individuals in my life. For years the Lord was telling me to set up firm boundaries with my mother. One mentor had told me to "wipe the dust off my feet" with my mother after every effort to make things right with her had appeared to fail. I had prayed and prayed, sought counsel and did whatever I honestly felt the Lord was telling me to do, from speaking to her about how I felt, writing her letters and praying for her. I even took my dad out for lunch one day to explain my emotional state and how I felt my mother's behavior was hurting me. That meeting ended extremely poorly too. I left bawling my eyes out. My dad completely ignored me, as I feel he always has. In his words, I am just a "spoiled brat."

I tried many things over many years, but each one felt like it blew up in my face. It was one slammed door after another. I was so discouraged, and my self-esteem suffered greatly. My emotional state worsened with every new blow. It was then, after watching me obediently follow the Lord to make things right with my mother, only to see me get beat up and kicked to the curb over and over again, my mentor gave me the word: it was time to wipe the dust off my feet and leave. He even offered for me to live in one of his rentals for free if it would help me escape the abuse and start my healing journey.

This mentor was a godly, spirit-filled man, and I do believe, especially now as I look back, that he was speaking the word of the Lord. However, I disobeyed. I was afraid of the judgment that would come from walking away. I wanted this relationship to work so badly. I love my mother and wanted her in my life. For ten more years I stayed, suffering more emotional abuse before I finally had the courage to listen. Finally a breaking point came, and I knew it had to be done. More than ready to focus on my healing I wiped the dust off and didn't look back.

It was like I finally could see clearly. *I will never earn this woman's love and respect. No matter what I do, she sees me as a bratty, spoiled, ungrateful child who needs to be emotionally beaten into submission.* Whether my mother is aware of her abusive ways or not, it is not my problem. I have completely released her to the Lord. She is God's child too. God made her just as he made me. God knows her way better than I do. He is the one who can see the hearts of every human. He is the one who judges the intentions of the heart. He is the one who will personally take our cases and investigate them on our behalf. My God knows me and He knows my mother; I will leave her in His capable hands. For the first time in my life I had to start practicing setting boundaries.

What Are Boundaries?

Simply put, boundaries are limits I set for myself in relationships on what behaviors are acceptable for me. We can have physical, mental, emotional and spiritual boundaries. According to Dr. Henry Cloud and Dr. John Townsend, "Emotional boundaries help us to deal with our own emotions and disengage from the harmful, manipulative emotions of others." Setting boundaries is incredibly healthy and is absolutely necessary for healing heart wounds and maintaining a healed heart.

Unfortunately, I had such a bad connotation with boundaries. The phrase "putting up walls" was used in a negative context so many times I was under the false impression all walls were bad, and therefore all boundaries were bad. As a result, I have struggled with this concept of boundaries more than other areas of my healing journey. Well, news flash to me, not having any walls is a recipe to be walked all over and hurt over and over and over again. Learning to set up boundaries to keep the right people in and the wrong people out was a must, even if that included my mother. Boundaries, I have learned, are especially necessary in toxic relationships, and I am not a bad person for having them.

Permission For Boundaries Granted

Many years ago a friend of mine, without knowing the relationship struggles I was having with my mother, lent me a life-changing book. It was one of those books you know God led her to lend me because it was exactly what I needed. The book was called *Boundaries* by Dr. Henry Cloud and Dr. John Townsend. If you haven't read it I highly recommend you do. It is very insightful. My biggest takeaway from this book was permission to set boundaries. Part of my struggle with obeying the Lord was I was stuck in the mindset that I was being hateful or ungrateful for setting up boundaries.

"Lord, where does this struggle with boundaries come from? The Lord began to show me images of my childhood. As these images played in my mind it me hit me all at once. My boundaries struggle was rooted in my childhood. Every image the Lord showed me was from a time when I was prevented from having a boundary I felt I needed. As a child I was not allowed to have boundaries. No wonder I struggled so much, but it was true.

One of the images the Lord showed me was of a time when I was fourteen; I moved out of the room I shared with my sister into a room in the basement. We had shared a room for ten years, so I was excited to have my own space. It wasn't a real room. It was probably more like an office. There was no closet and no door. My dad nailed a blanket up in the doorway to serve as a curtain, and then later installed an accordion door. Nevertheless, I loved it. It was my own space.

The basement phone was in this room as well. My own space *and* a phone...I don't think I could have been more excited. Not long after I moved into my new room I, sadly, learned what I thought was my own space really wasn't. It was more like a space where I was allowed to sleep and keep my stuff, but I had zero authority in the space and zero privacy. Any time the phone rang or if anyone in the house wanted to use the phone they were allowed to enter my room without knocking or announcing themselves. I quickly discovered I couldn't even change my clothes in this space without fearing family coming in at an inopportune time and seeing me inappropriately. The traffic in and out of my room was completely out of my control.

I asked everyone to knock first, and not one person respected my request. I addressed this issue with my parents frequently, but they did nothing to help me. There was no sympathy nor understanding of my privacy needs as a teenage girl with boys in the house. Every time I asked for rules to be put in place about knocking before entering my room my parents would remind me that it wasn't my room. I remember one night begging my parents to agree to have everyone to knock before entering. They sternly told me *no*. When I asked why, they replied it was because the phone in my room was a family phone and anyone was allowed to have access to it whenever they wanted. I suggested removing the phone from my room so it wasn't in there. Again they reminded me that it wasn't my room, and they wanted the phone in that room, end of discussion.

I was completely defeated. I didn't feel safe in my own home, and there was nowhere safe I could escape too. Trapped in my childhood home, I was living in a house where I wasn't respected. I wasn't allowed to make my own boundaries, and when I tried my parents made clear I didn't have that right. Both of my siblings had private rooms, but for some reason I wasn't allowed to.

My struggle with boundaries carried into adulthood only I didn't recognize it as a struggle until late in my twenties. With every rejection to my childhood attempts to make boundaries I noted in my subconscious that boundaries were wrong and they were a way to cut people off, which I also didn't have a right to do. Living without boundaries was a miserable way of living. I felt as if I couldn't say no to people and had to allow others to walk all over me. To become confident in who I was called to be, I needed to learn to make firm boundaries with those who are toxic.

Setting boundaries is a way of respecting other people as much as myself. They are a healthy way of living and can be adjusted to various circumstances. If we are clear with our boundaries with other people we are protecting them too – from possible anger and bitterness we may develop if we feel the other person is taking advantage of us. If our boundaries are not made clear the other person may have no idea we feel taken advantage of. This may result in an unnecessary friendship break, an awkward work environment or a mother-daughter separation.

Love With The Boundary

Don't play the blame game. Seriously, I have had too many mother-daughter battles firing missiles of words at each other starting with, "You always..." or "You never..." This is pointless and unproductive. I felt consistently disrespected, and I am sure my mother did too. I wish I knew how to set boundaries with my mother before we got to the point of angry outbursts. We all live and learn. I have been angry, frustrated and bitter towards my mother because she has hurt me, continued to hurt me and refuses to acknowledge she has been hurtful toward me. However, I have learned how to love myself. I no longer give her the power to hurt me. If she hurts me now it is only because I gave her that power, and that is my own fault. Having a firm boundary with her is loving myself, and I love my mom enough to release her from me. Boundaries are loving.

When we set clear boundaries with our mother we trust her to be mature enough to handle these boundaries appropriately. If she is not mature enough to do so we will learn quickly, and firmer boundaries will need to be set to protect our hearts. We cannot control the maturity of others, sadly. However, if our mother is mature enough to handle our boundaries, yet is struggling with keeping one or many it's a great opportunity for an open conversation where we can reach out and ask, "How can I help you be more successful in this?" And vice versa. Maybe there is an uncommunicated boundary of hers we have disrespected unknowingly. Honestly if we get to this point we are winning. We are on our way to a healthy relationship with our mother which would be a double win – a healed heart and a healed relationship. Score!

When setting boundaries you may have different levels of access for different people. When setting your boundaries ask yourself, "How safe are these people to my mental, emotional, spiritual and financial health?" Create your boundary accordingly. For example, some people, like my best friend and my children, have my permission to call me at any time day or night if they need me. However, a co-worker or client only has my permission to call during business hours. If they call after dinner I won't even bother picking up the phone because they have stepped over that boundary with me.

Now, boundaries do not have to be forever. If my mother has been super respectful of my boundary, our relationship seems to be improving and I feel more valued, then I would want to revisit my boundaries with her and reset them. However, before I enter that resetting boundary conversation I have decided in advance how much I am willing to let her in. Just because I am resetting our boundaries does not mean I am obligated to pull them way back or completely remove them all together.

This is my heart and my health. I am allowed to move at my own pace. If I need to take baby steps in this area, then I will without shame. There's no shame in setting boundaries. There is no shame in the rate in which I grow in them. And there is no shame in you growing in them. We are not bad people, and we are not cutting anyone off; we are protecting our hearts and health.

When my mother used to come and visit she would completely over take my kitchen, and I hated it. But my insecure self at that time did not know how to tell her. I didn't know how to set up healthy boundaries with my mom yet. When I attempted any kind of boundary with my mother she made me feel completely guilty and shameful for trying. When it comes to the kitchen I usually have meals planned ahead and a fully stocked pantry with everything in its place. I actually like cooking dinner for my family and trying new recipes.

Often when my mother came to visit she would assume her place in the kitchen. If I shared that I had a plan for dinner she would go out to buy chicken anyway. Then, not only does she buy chicken, she buys a cart full of groceries. I remind her that I had a plan to cook dinner, and she says, "I am sure you did," and continues bringing bag after bag from the car into my kitchen. Half the stuff she buys we either don't eat due to dietary needs or we prefer not to.

One time while helping my mother unload the dreaded groceries our conversation went something like, "Mom, we don't eat canned pineapple." She responds with, "It's always good to have one on hand." *What?* "Mom, we don't eat margarine." She answers, "It's cheaper than butter." The whole unloading of the groceries goes on like this. I am so annoyed. I really did try to communicate in my scaredy-cat, insecure way. My heart was so wounded I couldn't even tell her to stop with the groceries.

When I announced I was going to start making dinner my mother cut me off and tells me that she *thought* we could have chicken and she *just happened* to buy an overload of sides to go with it. Before I respond she begins to order me around in my own kitchen to help her prepare dinner. I hated every minute of this. Pretty much every meal went like this when she visited – some were worse. Like the time she took all my spices out of the cupboard, put them on the floor, plopped herself on the floor and began alphabetizing them. I asked her what she was doing, and she replied, "I don't know how you live like this."

This was just an example from my own relationship with my mother where set clear boundaries would have really been beneficial and healthy. I was too wounded to clearly communicate how what she was doing was hurting me. Even though her intentions may have been pure her delivery wasn't appreciated and felt disrespectful. I need to feel that I have control in my own home. At that time though I was still operating with wrong mindsets. I didn't know how to make my mother stop; I didn't know how to set boundaries.

Setting Boundaries

If you are like me, the most difficult part about setting boundaries is being able to put them into clear, understandable words. Wording can be so crucial. What I have learned is that it doesn't have to be pretty and professional. Just say it however it comes out; you can clean it up after by asking questions. You may want to start by saying, "This is where I am at right now…" and continue with, "This is how _____ is making me feel…" Then, give your mother the opportunity to correct her inappropriate, hurtful or just unwelcome behavior. When your mother does not change and it becomes a complete emotional disaster, it's not your imagination; she is toxic and damaging. To protect your physical, emotional, mental and spiritual health you have to escort them out of your life.

This is exactly the place I was at in my life. At one point my mother had crossed so many boundaries it was destroying me to have her in my life. The repeated offense was not okay. The only way I could get clarity on it all was to have her out of my life. In my mind this kind of boundary looks like a fence. At my house my rather large yard has a fence all around it. My mother has to stay outside the fence of my yard, of my domain. If she is going to damage my property she is no longer allowed on my property.

When I got to this point with my mother the letting go created so many mixed emotions. I felt like I had failed. I felt like I had failed my mother, failed our relationship, failed God and failed myself. Even though it was unhealthy I had let go of the hope that our relationship would ever be healthy. With all hope gone I found myself grieving the loss of a relationship I never really had. At the core I was grieving the loss of hope. My idea of having a wise older woman's council and support in my life was gone.

Setting this firm boundary was for me, and maybe this is what you have to do for you. We are doing this for ourselves because a healthy, joy-filled life is what we are called to. We are allowed to feel all the feels without anyone telling us how to feel. In the past my mother has taken it upon herself to tell me how I feel rather than asking. I don't know if she has ever honestly asked me how I was feeling. According to my mother I am always angry and selfish. Even when I was feeling content she would insist I was angry. If I would try to counter that and let her know how I was really feeling I'd only end up angry because she would not listen to me. She knew the buttons to press, the words that would trigger me and used them to remind me that, "You were born angry." This dagger she would throw at me told me I wasn't allowed to own my emotions nor express them. Reflecting on this now, I have so much compassion for my mother. She is clearly deeply wounded herself, and without her own heart healing she is incapable of loving me the way I was designed to be loved.

Boundaries Make Our Domain Clear

In the past we may have allowed our mothers to dictate our emotions, but now we know our emotions are part of the domain *we rule over*. When we root ourselves deeply in the Word of God some of the natural fruit that is produced includes self-control, love, joy and peace (Gal. 5:22-23). Anger is not on the list. No one gets to tell us what kind of fruit we are going to produce. We choose where we plant our roots, and our fruit is the product of the roots. If we want to produce good fruit we plant ourselves in good soil. Our mother is not the soil we were meant to be planted in. Planting ourselves in someone else's soil will get us the rotting, stinky fruit we have already experienced the majority of our lives. We should not let anyone control our emotions and feelings. Let's plant ourselves in the truth of God's Word. Again, our emotions are our domain not our mother's or anyone else's.

I just need to share this one last thing about boundaries because I truly believe it was a gift from the Lord. While reading through Proverbs 8 during my morning Bible time God highlighted this scripture:

> "...when he set in place the pillars of the earth
> and spoke the decrees of the seas,
> commanding the waves
> so that they wouldn't overstep their boundaries..."
> Proverbs 8:29 (TPT)

If you ever felt like boundaries were like unwanted walls re-read this scripture. God purposefully gave the seas a boundary. The boundary of the seas and oceans are the shores. The waves crash on those shores, but our God the Creator has commanded them not to pass those shores. When you look at the shore of a sea do you see a wall? No! You see a beautiful sandy beach. In some places you may see a wall of rocks, but when I read this scripture I pictured a beautiful sandy shore. The waves crash on it, and then roll back into the sea. The boundary is healthy and protects the land and everything on the land. When the sea oversteps its boundary there can be catastrophic results. Depending on the strength and size of the overstepping there can be slight damage or catastrophic disaster. Whether the boundary be for the ocean or our mothers, immense damage can happen when the limits they are given are not respected. Isn't that a great image? I love it. It is such a beautiful illustration of the boundary and a great reminder to all of us that boundaries are natural and originate with God.

Unboxed Prayer

Abba,

Thank you so much for the revelation of boundaries. I ask that You show me where in my life I need to set up healthy boundaries to protect my heart, emotional, mental and spiritual health. You are such a good, good Father who loves us unconditionally. Give me the boldness I need to set up every boundary and the wisdom to set them up according to Your Word.

I love You, Papa God, AMEN!

· NINE ·

Wisdom, My Passionate Pursuit

It was Christmas morning and my husband and I sat on the couch in our Kansas City apartment with my parents on speaker phone. It was my first Christmas in the United States since immigrating from Canada. Yet, it was my second Christmas in a row away from family (we spent almost a year in China before moving to the United States). Also, my husband and I had a baby during our stay in China, and no one in my family had met our new little addition. We had only been in the United States for a few months and we were desperately trying to stabilize our lives in our new home. So this holiday had a lot of mixed emotions with wanting to be with loved ones and show off my new bundle of joy, while trying to make a new life in a new country, away from everything familiar and having no one to help navigate it.

We had hardly anything when we first arrived to Kansas from China, but we came full of hope and faith that our Heavenly Father would provide. When we first got our apartment it was still empty even with everything we owned in it. I remember laying sleeping bags and blankets on the floor, trying to arrange them to look as inviting as possible. I wanted it to look nice even though we were sleeping on the floor. From different members of the church we attended we received donations of a couch, desk and table, but no bed.

One day, a sweet man from church approached us and asked if we had a bed yet, and we sadly replied, "No." He went on to say that he saw a queen-sized mattress out by the dumpster where he lived. He even smelled it, and it "smelled fine." If we were interested he would bring it by. Our young, desperate selves cried, "Yes!" Looking back on this now I am grossed out by my own story, however I remember just being thankful that we could get off the hard, uncomfortable floor.

With that dumpster mattress we were starting to feel settled. Our baby slept in a playpen, our three-year-old slept with us and my husband, within a month and a half of arriving in Kansas City, was able to start working three different jobs. Each job had entry-level pay, so even though my husband seemed to be working all the time we were struggling to pay the bills each month. Even still, I was thankful and with each passing day things were looking brighter. I was so full of hope that this season was only temporary. I knew we were going to make it.

Now here we were, having only been in the United States for three months, wishing my parents a Merry Christmas over the phone. I hadn't seen them in close to 18 months. Earlier in the year my parents had planned a Hawaiian trip around the same time my wonderful little family was making their way from China to the United States. I remember trying to work out the finances to see if I could coordinate meeting up with them in Hawaii on our way from China to the United States, but there was no way I could make those finances work. It was going to cost too much money to try to fit that little side trip into our journey. All I really wanted was for my parents to meet my daughter. My heart ached for them to see her. When I suggested to my parents that they meet us in Kansas instead, they reminded me of their bi-annual tradition of vacationing in Hawaii. When I asked for them to make an exception just for this year so they could meet their grandchild, they declined and replied, "This is what we do." Even though my heart ached I accepted it. I knew that would be the outcome, but it didn't hurt to try. Honestly I wasn't offended, just a little sad.

While we talked on the phone sharing about our day and what we had planned, my parents said, "I am sure you noticed we didn't send you a Christmas gift; we wanted to tell you what your gift was over the phone." They continued, "We will pay for plane tickets for

178

your family to join us in Hawaii. You will have to cover your expenses once we are there, but we will pay for your tickets." My husband and I were shocked...not in the good kind of way. We stared at each other in silence, not knowing what to say. "So, start saving your money," my mother encouraged.

We couldn't stop staring at each other, like we were trying to find the words to say in each other's eyes. The words wouldn't come. I don't even remember what I said in response; I just remember how I felt. I felt like I had just been kicked in the stomach and told "Merry Christmas." The people who I longed to feel loved by, seen and supported, were already planning their next Hawaiian trip, when they literally had just gone to Hawaii that fall. This couple I ached to share my children with and have them meet their newest grandchild had Hawaii on their mind. *Do they even want to meet their grandchild? Do they care about their grandchild?* I was so confused and hurt. And to tell us to start saving money? We are sleeping on a mattress that was pulled from a dumpster, and my mother tells us to start saving money for Hawaii.

As soon as we hung up my husband and I looked at each other as if we knew what the other was thinking. I don't remember who broke the silence, but one of us said, "We aren't going." We were both in agreement that when we got to a point when we were able to start saving money, it wouldn't be for a Hawaiian vacation. It would be for a down payment on a house so we could get out of the renting game. We had a goal of being home owners someday...and bed owners.

My husband saw the familiar guilt come over my face as it did when I felt obligated to do what my mother wanted me to do even though it felt wrong in my spirit. He gently reminded me of every previous time we spent our vacation to visit my parents. Each of those visits turned into fierce spiritual battles against manipulation, control, gaslighting and other forms of unconscious witchcraft. They were strains on our relationship, and we always left those visits exhausted, frustrated, hurt and defeated. There had been no indication this visit in Hawaii would be any different; we would just be in a vacation spot with two toddlers and a financial component to add to it. Even the brief moments I entertained the idea of going felt stressful. My husband wisely brought light to the fact that we are meant to learn from our past, not repeat it.

As I meditate on this memory I am reminded of this scripture:

"As a dog returns to its vomit, so fools repeat their folly.
Do you see a person wise in their own eyes?
There is more hope for a fool than for them."
Proverbs 26:11-12 (NIV)

The Lord used this moment to show me that I have been the fool. My whole life I kept returning to the presence of my mother, compromising what I felt in my spirit in an attempt to be a "good" daughter and continually partnering with the lie, "Maybe this time will be different." I kept living the same way, but hoping for different results. I was a fool. It was time to listen to the voice of wisdom. My husband and I politely declined the plane tickets to Hawaii and it felt really good. We knew it was the wise thing to do.

What Is Wisdom?

According to dictionary.com, wisdom is defined as, "The quality or state of being wise; knowledge of what is true or right coupled with just judgment as to action; sagacity, discernment, or insight." Wise, as defined by dictionary.com, is "having the power of discerning and judging properly as to what is true or right; possessing discernment, judgment, or discretion." Where, exactly, does this power come from, and how can it be useful in our healing journeys?

Many would agree that wisdom comes from life's experiences and helps us to make wiser or more educated and more aware decisions in and for our future. However, in the Bible our ability to attain and apply wisdom is directly related to our relationship to God and His Word. There is no better place to start pursuing wisdom for our lives than the book of Proverbs. Proverbs is a well-known biblical book about wisdom. The wisdom found in Proverbs is meant to lead and guide us in every aspect of our lives, including relationships.

Honestly I never really dove into the book of Proverbs until recently. I would read a verse here and there but never took the time to really study Scripture and learn how to apply it to my life. I did not see the significance of it, and since I am being honest I struggled with some of the verses especially the ones about mothers. Some didn't seem to apply to me. For example, Proverbs 31:26: "Her teachings are filled with wisdom and kindness as loving instruction pours from her lips" (TPT). Or Proverbs 31:28: "Her sons and daughters arise in one accord to extol her virtues" (TPT). I would read things like this and, due to the relationship I had with my mother, would think *Nope!*

It is sad to think my relationship with my mother kept me from embracing wisdom and allowing it to soak into me and guide me. Proverbs is so rich with wisdom, we all need to read it, believe it and apply it. There is so much more than meets the eye in this little book.

For me, two things tore down every wall I had erected against the book of Proverbs. First, looking up the meaning of the word Proverb to understand it better, and second was hearing Dr. Brian Simmons share how the mother and father written about in Proverbs are not referring to my earthly parents.

Discovering the meaning of the word "proverb" shattered my preconceived ideas about the book of Proverbs and drew me into itself. It is now my most consistently read book in Bible. I want to get to the depths of every word, understand it to the fullest and have my life reflect it.

The word *proverb* has several layers to it. The most common meaning is, "a parable or saying." However, the meaning that burst through my preconceived wall like water shooting through a manmade dam was found at biblestudytools.com. "The word is just as likely to be connected with the verb *mashal*, 'to rule' or 'master.'" As soon as this definition was revealed to me the Holy Spirit immediately reminded me of our original purpose at creation: to rule and to reign our own dominion. This revelation unfolded in an instant. God gave us dominion in the Garden of Eden, and it was His intent that we rule over it. With this definition exposed it became evident to me the book of Proverbs is there as an aid to help us rule and master over our God-given domains and to take back the authority the devil stole from us. This revelation empowered me, encouraged me and gave me confidence in my previous boundary-setting actions.

My mother may no longer have authority in my life unless I give it to her. She thought she had the right to come into my house, tell me how to feel, tell me how to arrange my spices, tell me what groceries I should buy, and tell my son how to fix his hair. Yet I cannot completely blame her. She thought she had that right and authority because I let her. I did not know when I moved out of my parents' house, set up my own place and paid all my own bills there was an authority shift. I was never taught that I had stepped out in my own domain and that I was responsible to rule and reign it. Many years later I was still allowing my mom to waltz into my domain and reign it. Because I didn't know about setting up boundaries I didn't exercise my authority in my domain. It was my house, my kitchen, my spices, my children, and my feelings, but I wasn't acting like it.

The book of Proverbs is the guide book I had all along and didn't even know it. As I spend time in Proverbs and build a relationship with Wisdom I am led and guided in the ways of the Most High on how to rule and reign my domain. I am given strategies to be successful in the life my Father in Heaven has for me.

Listening to Dr. Brian Simmons, the creator of The Passion Translation, teach on the book of Proverbs was life changing. I still remember listening while in the basement of one of my previous homes and being blown away at the thought that the father and mother written about in Proverbs wasn't actually talking about my earthly parents. Just knowing this helps heal my heart from daddy wounds. And all those scriptures referring to a mother isn't speaking of *my* emotionally abusive mother, whom I need firm boundaries with. It was like a weight lifted off of my shoulders. The tension I had with this book vanished in an instant, and it was no longer the book that contained shame and guilt; it was a loving guide designed for me to aid in bettering my life and helping me succeed. I had never seen the Proverbs in this light before, and it was freeing.

In Proverbs Solomon speaks as father, a good and loving father. This is metaphorical of our Father in Heaven. As we read we can picture our Heavenly Father loving us through His guidance and imparting His wisdom in us. He does this because He is a Father who desires us to be successful, abundantly successful. He knows wisdom will protect us in this life: it will protect our hearts, our minds and our emotions. And wisdom will lead us into abundance, the kind of abundance that will draw others closer to Him. I am imagining abundance not in material things, but an abundance in joy, love, peace, kindness, confidence, supernatural life strategies, success, healthy relationships, energy, knowledge, and understanding.

Metaphorically in Proverbs our mother is the church. When I say church I am not talking about the possible toxic environments we may have experienced in the past. I am not talking about people who have abused their power of authority and have hurt us or others in the name of God. I am not talking about the country clubs that call themselves churches full of feel-good speeches and exclusive, clicky get-togethers. I am not talking about the kind of church your mother and my mother may go to or raised us in. You know, the kind that may be full of people who may be narcissistic, gaslighting, manipulative, lying, exaggerating, feeling powerful while making others feel disempowered, yet encouraging each other and justify their actions because they are "good" people and do "good" things for the church. No, no and NO!

I am speaking of the genuine body of Christ. Those who have an active relationship with Jesus who receive and apply the whole Word of God, not just bits and pieces of it or only the parts they like. No! The genuine church practices forgiveness, repentance and pursues more and more of God and His Word; they are never satisfied. They are like a fire that cannot be quenched. The genuine church is committed to the making of disciples, practicing inner healing, keeping each other accountable, loving each other with His love, listening to each other, praying for each other, interceding for Israel, the church, and for the lost. The genuine body of Christ understands we are part of a Kingdom and strive to think and act with a Kingdom mindset. This is our mother. She is not a building; she is a Kingdom. She doesn't give birth to bondage, but gives birth to freedom. She is the New Jerusalem (Galatians 4).

The church as our mother provides us with a healthy attachment to the body. It uses discernment to tune into our emotions, validate our pain and helps with our basic needs when necessary. It nurtures us, teaches us to connect to the heart of the Father, it corrects us and rebukes us lovingly with the strong desire for us to be blessed and fulfill Jesus' purpose for us. Wherever our earthly mothers failed us the genuine body of Christ fills. Seeing the church as our mother, these scriptures no longer stir up negative emotions in me.

Proverbs 31:26 says, "Her teachings are filled with wisdom and kindness as loving instruction pours from her lips" (TPT). This scripture now makes me think of every Spirit-filled teacher I have had. Without their loving instructions I would not be where I am today; I would not even be writing this book. Also read Proverbs 31:28: "Her sons and daughters arise in one accord to extol her virtues" (TPT). My thoughts immediately go to every believer, and this passage feels so beautifully prophetic which is a huge shift from the shame I felt before. Can you see why this was so mind blowing for me? I pray that you are also getting your own revelation right now concerning Proverbs and wisdom.

Throughout Proverbs we see wisdom as a woman. Recognizing this has personified Wisdom for me. Seeing Wisdom as a feminine person shows how Wisdom is meant for a relationship. We are to interact with Wisdom and make Wisdom a partner in life. The book of Proverbs was not meant to add to our academic knowledge about God and His ways; it is meant to lead us into a relationship with Wisdom. In this relationship the revelational truths about God, His Kingdom and who we are will be revealed to our hearts for the purpose of transforming us as we apply it to our lives.

How Can We Apply Wisdom?

Like every other relationship, in order for our relationship with Wisdom to be healthy, growing and producing abundant good fruit we need to spend time in the presence of God. Listen to His wisdom, read and study His Proverbs, enter into conversations about these verses with Him, ask questions, walk and talk, pause and listen. When we spend time with the Lord, seeking His wisdom, it will absorb into our beings. The more time we spend soaking with the Lord and His wisdom, His thought patterns will become our thought patterns. In this way, walking with Wisdom becomes a lifestyle. Dance with Wisdom, run with Wisdom, do the dishes with Wisdom, do life with Wisdom. Above all else never stop pursuing Wisdom like we should never stop pursuing the ones we love.

To eliminate any possible confusion with pursuing a relationship with Wisdom and pursuing a relationship with Jesus, the scriptures say they are one and the same. We are not pursuing two separate relationships.

"But it is from Him that you are in Christ Jesus, who became to us wisdom from God [revealing His plan of salvation], and righteousness [making us acceptable to God], and sanctification [making us holy and setting us apart for God], and redemption [providing our ransom from the penalty for sin]..."
1 Corinthians 1:30 (AMP)

This scripture makes it clear: Jesus is our wisdom. Pursuing a relationship with Jesus is pursuing a relationship with Wisdom. We cannot separate the two. Jesus is Wisdom made into a person. It is also easier for us to actively pursue a relationship when we can envision a person.

Solomon, The Wisest Man To Ever Live

Since wisdom is about applying God's truth, where do we go from here?

"And if anyone longs to be wise, ask God for wisdom and he will give it! He won't see your lack of wisdom as an opportunity to scold you over your failures but he will overwhelm your failures with his generous grace." James 1:5 (TPT)

King Solomon, the son of King David, was most known for his wisdom and has been called the wisest man to ever live. He is also the author of Proverbs. It is very important for us to understand how Solomon acquired all his wisdom. It didn't come from focused studying or life experiences and he wasn't born with it. No, one night the Lord appeared to Solomon in a dream. In this dream the Lord asked Solomon what he wanted from God. This is what Solomon replied:

"Then Solomon said, 'You have shown Your servant David my father great lovingkindness, because he walked before You in faithfulness and righteousness and with uprightness of heart toward You; and You have kept for him this great lovingkindness, in that You have given him a son to sit on his throne, as it is today. So now, O Lord my God, You have made Your servant king in place of David my father; and as for me, I am but a little boy [in wisdom and experience]; I do not know how to go out or come in [that is, how to conduct business as a king]. Your servant is among Your people whom You have chosen, a great people who are too many to be numbered or counted. So give Your servant an understanding mind *and* a hearing heart [with which] to judge Your people, so that I may discern between good and evil. For who is able to judge *and* rule this great people of Yours?'" 1 Kings 3: 6-9 (AMP)

We will focus on the last part of King Solomon's answer, however let's first read the progression of his answer leading up to the request. King Solomon understood his father was a great king and had favor with the Lord. Being the man to fill his father's footsteps he knew he needed supernatural equipping that could only come from the Lord, whom his father walked with. Solomon requests, "an understanding mind *and* a hearing heart [with which] to judge Your people, so that I may discern between good and evil." In short, King Solomon asks God for wisdom. Remember, wisdom is defined as, "The quality or state of being wise; knowledge of what is true or right coupled with just judgment as to action; sagacity, discernment, or insight" (dictionary.com). Notice how Solomon recognized God as the source. He also had a humble opinion of himself as we see when he referred to himself as a child. Solomon pursued wisdom because his heart's desire was to be a good king, walking in the ways of the Lord.

The Lord granted Solomon his request and added great wealth. Solomon's reputation of overwhelming wisdom spread throughout the known world. When the Queen of Sheba heard about Solomon's wisdom she had to make the trip to see for herself. When you walk in great wisdom people are drawn to you and you have the opportunity to lead others to the source of your wisdom. If Solomon was just a kind, loving king people would not have taken notice and certainly not travelled great distances to be in his presence. When your life is abundantly blessed you are successful in everything you put your hand to. Your finances are not stressful, your family is genuinely joy filled, and when your life is working beautifully the people around you take notice. People begin to ask, "Why are you so full of joy? Why are you so successful? How is your family so peaceful? How?" People will ask, and that is when you point them to the source of your abundance.

Our source is our Heavenly Father, our Creator, our Provider, our King, and the King of Kings. Our lives are a testimony. When we are in an intimate relationship with Wisdom it will be noticeable. You don't even have to try. Life in relationship with Wisdom sets you apart from the world. As you succeed in life through the guidance of Wisdom you have the responsibility to point every one of those people to the source of your success. I love this quote from Myles Munroe: "Your success is good for God." Solomon's life became a testimony for the greatness of God, and so can ours.

Trust In God And His Timing

Our God is not a genie in a bottle. We don't rub the Bible three times or follow a secret formula, make a wish and be instantly gratified. It doesn't work like that. God is still God and has the authority to work in His timing, not ours. Interestingly enough God's timing is always the better timing. What we think may be the right timing, time often proves that it wasn't. We need to trust that God sees the bigger picture. He sees the past, present and the future. He is also all-knowing and we are not. Trusting God for the timing relieves the pressures of control. Some things are not in our control, and therefore we need to remain humble before the Father, leaving whatever it is in His hands and choose to forget about it. When God wants to deal with it He will.

This also applies to wisdom. When we pray for wisdom it will most likely not happen as it did for Solomon. Solomon was granted an overwhelming amount of wisdom. We need to be aware that God gives wisdom in His timing and in His measures, and we need to be okay with that. I believe as we are responsible with the wisdom God gives us, applying it generously to our lives, yielding our ways to walk in God's way, He will release more to us. As we grow and mature in our relationship with Jesus so will our wisdom grow. With that said, let us humble ourselves like a child, eager to absorb the ways of Wisdom in whatever timing and whatever measures the Lord chooses.

There is wisdom in God's timing. I am preaching to myself right now. As I reflect on my own life I see my broken spirit of a person trying to force my own way because I didn't feel God was working fast enough. So many closed doors when I begged for them to open. So many failed attempts to create a relationship that hasn't happened yet. So much searching for a place that felt like home, for a place where I felt free and I had permission to be me. So many empty spaces in my spirit I didn't know how to fill.

About 20 years ago I was on my knees so hungry to be loved; I wanted to physically feel the arms of my Heavenly Father holding me. I desperately wanted to feel His presence in such a tangible way I would instantly be made whole. Every part of me wanted to melt away so that my spirit would come fully alive. Yet every time I looked up it was as if I was looking at Jesus through an ice wall. I was so close, He was right there, but I couldn't touch Him, I couldn't feel Him. I could just see He was there. I begged God to give me the strength to chip through this ice to be with Him. Like I begged God to fix the relationship with my mom, neither has happened the way I wanted it to or in the timing.

During that same time I had some of the most powerful spiritual experiences with God. I was never satisfied with those experiences though; I wanted more of Him. There was more to have. I could see it. It just wasn't His timing for me to have that level of intimacy. Later I had a revelation that those deeply spiritual experiences were glimpses of who God made me to be and the life I was made for. Those glimpses were the hope I had to trust God for His timing.

I will admit while waiting for the breakthrough my attitude has not always been the best. *This is taking too long.* Not to mention I seriously get distracted too easily. The thing was, I wasn't participating in my breakthrough. I would have moments of participation, but really I was just frustrated for being stuck in the wilderness, stuck behind the ice wall. Now I understand I wasn't ready for that kind of breakthrough. I needed the time in the wilderness to prepare me for the breakthrough.

The Lord further revealed that I have felt so stuck because I wasn't obedient. For example, God told me to write this book over ten years ago. TEN! But I let fear and daily distractions become my excuse for not writing. Then, this year the Lord began to move me out of my wilderness. Doors I have longed to open suddenly opened, and a lot of exciting change happened in a very short period of time. The way life was moving it was unmistakably God. Then, came the urgency to write this book. It was an incredible urgency followed by two words from two different people who didn't know me, both saying, "Whatever God has you working on you are to finish by the end of the year."

I do not know what kind of plans God has for this book; even if the whole point of it was to test my obedience and to lead me out of my own wilderness, then that is enough. If the only thing that comes out of this is a closer walk with my Father in Heaven I am good with it. My prayer, though, is for God to use this book to draw others closer to Himself, advance His Kingdom and glorify His name.

The children of God wandered in the wilderness for 40 years fighting their own battles of survival; they were forced to trust God and His timing. As unpleasant as the wilderness was and how easy it was to complain about the circumstances what they didn't realize was God was preparing them for another battle. The Promised Land was theirs for the taking, but that's just it: they had to take it. The children of God didn't just walk into the land and claim it, they had to fight for it. They went to war when they got their promise (Joshua 6). The years we have been in bondage to our mothers was our wilderness. We felt as if we were fighting just to survive in that abusive environment. And we have battled really hard for our hearts to be healed, our minds to be renewed and positioning ourselves for revelation truth.

In God's timing we will be led out of our wilderness and into our promise. I feel like every person reading this book is on the edge of

190

the wilderness, just steps away from their promise. When you do step out of your wilderness and into your promise know that your battles are not over. It is not a free and easy ride from here. The battles are sure to come, but know that the promised land battles are different from the wilderness battles. God is breaking us completely of our wilderness mindset, the "survival mode" mindset. Now we are taking back what's supposed to be ours in the first place. And for this special task we need a conquering mindset. We are taking ownership of our domain and preparing to guard it fiercely. Do not skip over or rush through developing your relationship with Wisdom. You will need the guidance from your intimacy to help you guard and rule your domain.

To give another picture of expecting different battles after the wilderness here is a sports illustration. When I was in school I loved playing basketball. I always looked forward to basketball tryouts at the beginning of the school year. The adrenaline and excitement of the sport helped me prepare for the tryouts. Depending on the competition you sometimes had to work very hard just to make the team. For professional sports teams athletes go through intense training for years before they get an invitation to try out. These athletes battle for a spot on the team.

When they finally make the team they can't stop working. They don't stop fighting the battles; the focus of the battle has just changed. Now these athletes work hard to stay off the bench and be a starter. Then, they are battling for wins, and then championships. The battles and hard work do not stop. If you want the reward of being a great and recognized athlete you will always be battling and working; it does not stop until you retire.

Have The Mind Of A Conqueror

You are about to break free from the wilderness. Expect more battles. Stay close to Wisdom and you will conquer each one. In preparation for the coming battles you will need Wisdom to understand the moments – to know when to speak, when to be quiet, when to move and when to stay, when to push through and when to wait. Also I encourage you to speak things as they will be, not as you see them right now. Do not glorify the devil and all his hard work to keep you in the wilderness. Keep your mouth from negative speech. Stop yourself from pointing out all your flaws, fails and wounds. Speak of your healing, the wonderful work God has done in your heart, brag of His great work in your life, share the revelations our Father has given you, praise the Lord for leading you out of the wilderness and into your promise. Praise the Lord for every victory you have had and are going to have. You may even want to speak of your boundaries out loud for a bit, knowing it is okay to have boundaries; doing this may even help you become more comfortable with them when you say it and hear it. Speak life over yourself.

Finally, with Wisdom you will need to perform regular self-maintenance – the things we do to keep ourselves in a right relationship with Wisdom. This would include being aware of our habits and choosing to be intentional about self-correction where needed. It can kind of be like showering. We don't just shower once and call ourselves clean for the rest of our lives. That would be disgusting! In the same way, with Wisdom guiding you, schedule self-maintenance times. This could include a self-reflection time at the end of the day right before you go to bed. Sit on your bed and ask the Father, "Is there anything in my heart that needs correcting? Did anything happen today that I need to deal with?" Listen to what the Holy Spirit says to your heart and obey immediately. For those like me, I need little reminders; writing little notes to myself helps. You may want to write yourself a little note and leave it near your bed where you will see it, reminding you to have these conversations with Your Father before going to sleep for the night.

Self-Maintenance Suggestions

Listen to teachings by Spirit-filled, God-fearing teachers

Have a moment of silence every morning when you wake up, no music, no tv, and no noise, just silence and listen. If God wants to impart something in you, He will.

Mediate on Scripture.

Memorize Scripture.

Write a list of all the things you are thankful for, and post it in a place where you see it.

Make a list of all the things you love about yourself. You are a child of God, pay attention to the beauty of His art.

Have a solo worship time, just you dancing and singing before your God.

If you play and instrument, schedule times to play it. Make up new songs in worship to the Father. And have fun with it.

Take a walk in nature, do this as frequently as possible.

Pick a biblical topic and study it. Ask the Lord what topic He wants you to research; you may be surprised by His answer.

Have a 'You and God' weekend. Get a hotel room, bring a Bible and a notebook and just spend time with God. Do this especially when you start feeling disconnected.

Call a friend from your inner circle, the kind who celebrates you. No complaining, no gossiping, no people shedding, just pure friendship fellowship.

Anyway, I could go on, but I think you should add some of your own things to this list. You know you. Whatever you do, never stop pursuing a relationship with Wisdom.

Unboxed Prayer

Father in Heaven,
You have set me apart for Your powerful purposes. I pray that You increase my discernment and wisdom so that I will clearly see the difference between Your ways and the sneaky ways of the devil. I want to be able to walk in wisdom without any concern about what the world thinks. Your ways are higher, Your ways are better. Keep my heart ignited for You, and may I always remain in a relationship with Wisdom, surrounded by Your presence.
In the mighty name of Jesus, AMEN!

TEN

Confidence, My Original Design

Feeling the presence of the Lord, interacting with the Holy Spirit and being aware of the spiritual atmosphere was always normal for me. However, what was as real to me as the physical realm was not accepted or understood by those closest to me growing up, including my mother. I had no one to guide me, instruct me, counsel me or comfort me as a child in this area. This resulted in conflicting and confusing thoughts about who I was and how I was supposed to fit into society.

As a little girl I remember lying in my bed at night and feeling Jesus come into the room and kiss me on the cheek. I remember feeling completely at peace, full of love and safe, knowing Jesus Himself was watching over me. When I told my mom of Jesus visiting me it was brushed off as either a dream or my imagination. I would strongly sense something in the spiritual realm, such as a caution, an uneasiness, a fakeness, a strict binding feeling, or sometimes pick up on a person's anger or bitterness, but it would feel like a suffocating blanket. And I would also feel overwhelming joy and peace at times. I would try to communicate the best I knew how, only to be misunderstood and called judgmental or too sensitive. When no one else was sharing what I sensed it always led me to the conclusion that something was wrong with me. *Why can't I blindly and effortlessly participate in all aspects of life without a care in the world.* It seemed as though everyone else could.

I remember one time at about 12 years old reading my Bible on my bed as I often did. I loved reading the Bible. This particular time I was reading in 1 Corinthians and had one of my first revelations.

The Holy Spirit came upon me and highlighted verse 4:10: "We are fools for Christ, but you are so wise in Christ! We are weak, but you are strong! You are honored, we are dishonored!"

The words, *I am a fool for Christ* started going on repeat in my head. Then I started to say those words out loud, "I am a fool for Christ." As I spoke it, a deep sense of understanding came over me and I began to get excited. My entire being was being filled with joy, and I loved what I was experiencing. Suddenly this verse was no longer just words on a page; it became a living understanding that I didn't have to worry about what anyone else thought of me. I was called to be His, to belong and to serve Jesus with all that I am. To the world I was going to look very foolish, but that was more than okay; I was excited to be the fool for Christ.

For the first time in my memory I became so filled with overwhelming joy and excitement. This new, deeper understanding of the scriptures gave me insight and clarity about my identity and pierced through the confusion that had camped out in my head. I just had to tell someone. This was how excited I was, I had to share this!

I went running out of my room, down the hall and into the kitchen, looking for anyone to share this revelation with. I found my mom working in the kitchen, and with a great big grin on my face and my body shaking with excitement, I blurted out, "I AM A FOOL FOR CHRIST!"

My mother sharply turned her head toward me and sternly replied, "We do not talk like that in this house." I stood there baffled and not sure how to respond. I literally just had an encounter with the Living God whose Holy Spirit led me into a revelation of His Holy Word…and I was being scolded for sharing. I was growing up in what I knew to be a "Christian" home. My parents religiously took our family to church every Sunday and believed the Bible to be true, so I wasn't understanding the problem. I must have looked completely confused by her reaction because my mother repeated herself. When I finally replied I remember saying, "But that is what the Bible says." I proved it using my Bible, and yet my mother's response still was, "Well, that is not how I take it. And we will not talk like that in this house."

"Talk like what?" I questioned.

"We are not fools, and we do not use that word in this house," she answered.

"But I am talking about being a fool for Christ," I insisted.

"A fool believes that there is no God, so we will not call anyone a fool in this house."

I tried to explain my revelation, but she would hear none of it. Not only would she not hear of it, her response made me feel as if I was not allowed to share the revelation with anyone because of the use of the word fool. I walked back to my room again confused. Who was I? Every time felt as if I began to head down the right path to discover my purpose and identity I felt disassembled back to pieces without and instruction manual to put them together.

Unfortunately this was not an isolated event. Revelations of Scripture, dreams, visions, Holy-Spirit encounters, hearing the voice of God, prophecy, praying in the Spirit, speaking God's Word, everything that made me feel normal, alive, joy filled, excited, and fulfilling my purpose seemed to be the very things that were taboo in my childhood home and community. Of course this deepened the confusion about my identity, purpose and place in this world. Trying to "fit in" and be who I felt I was supposed to be made life miserable. Being myself, I felt unaccepted, bullied and shamed. Trying to find middle ground made me feel fake. I wondered if the confusion would ever stop and if I would find my place in this world.

I want to share one more story, not because this is just another example of being confused about my identity or because I want you to connect with another sob story and feel validated in your own or validate me in mine. No! I want to share this next story because it is a prime example of how the enemy uses those closest ones to us to muzzle us. The enemy does not want us finding out who we are especially those who are called to speak truth, change atmospheres and to draw others closer to Jesus with our words.

This time I was 18 years old and had recently returned home from a six-month, life transforming training school with YWAM, Youth With A Mission. YWAM gave me the permission I had sought my whole life to seek God with everything I had and to embrace, with all my excitement and joy, every encounter God chose to have with me during that time. For the first time I received instruction, guidance and validation for my experiences with God. I wasn't crazy and there was nothing wrong with me. YWAM provided leaders to walk with me as I navigated and embraced my identity for the first time without a sense of shame. I had the freedom to run with my limitless God and soar as high as He would allow me to go. For the first time in my life I felt like I fit in. I had found a family that loved who I was made to be and encouraged me to be all I was purposed for.

During my YWAM time I was sitting on my bed one day reading the Bible. I had just finished reading 1 Corinthians 12-14 because I was curious about the spiritual gifts. Spiritual gifts seemed to be one of those taboo topics that no one talked about growing up, and I certainly don't remember any teachings of any kind about them. Here at YWAM though spiritual gifts were fully embraced, and I found myself on a steep learning curve. I wanted to learn all I could.

A verse was highlighted to me during this particular reading session: 1 Corinthians 14:1. "Follow the way of love and eagerly desire gifts of the Spirit, especially prophecy." Specifically, "eagerly desire gifts of the Spirit" really stood out. I began to talk with God and asked Him what 'eagerly desire' looked like. I also asked God, "If we are supposed to eagerly desire gifts of the Spirit, why haven't I been taught on this before? Why have I not seen this demonstrated? How do I eagerly desire the gifts of the Spirit?" I had so many questions.

Almost immediately after I asked and paused to listen the Lord responded with, "Pick one and ask Me for it." Surprised and excited, I quickly looked at the list of gifts and chose the gift of tongues. Right then I started to pray and ask God to give me the gift of tongues. I was hopeful that it would flow out of me the minute I asked, but

198

nothing happened.

The next morning one of the YWAM staff members picked me up for church. It was supposed to be a shuttle for any YWAMer who wanted to go to church, but this particular morning I was the only one on it. I hopped into the vehicle and away we went. As I rode along the driver started to share his testimony of how he received the gift of tongues. He just started sharing his long testimony out of the blue. He shared all the way to church, maybe a good 20 minutes, and didn't finish. As he dropped me off he said, "I will finish the story on the way home."

True to his word, the driver picked up right where he left off on our way home from church. His testimony ended right as we pulled up to my house. When the driver stopped the vehicle and realized he'd spent the entire time we were in the vehicle talking, he looked at me and said, "I have no idea why I told you that whole story. Maybe you were supposed to hear it. I don't know if you are seeking the gift of tongues or not, but I feel I am to tell you to ask and to not stop asking. You are to pray and ask for the gift of tongues every day until you receive it."

With that word, I thanked the driver and headed into my house, speechless. That driver had no idea of the conversation I had with God just the day before. I knew God had prompted him to tell me that story, and the message at the end was God talking to me. I was so excited. God was revealing Himself to me in a new way, and I was loving every minute of it. I did not waste any time. As soon as I got back to my room I got down on my knees and prayed for the gift of tongues.

Faithful with my daily prayer, after 30 days I was getting discouraged. I didn't understand why the gift had not come yet when I was being obedient. Little did I know my answer was on its way. On my bed talking with God again, I decided to get my discouragement out by writing in my journal. I had recently received a care package from my mother, and inside was a nice set of new gel pens to go with my journal. I reminded God of my obedience in asking for the gift of tongues every day. I wrote, "Why have I not received it yet?" As soon as I finished writing that sentence I heard the word, "Pray." I stopped writing and looked around the room. The only one there, I wondered *am I imagining something?*

I shrugged it off and returned to writing in my journal, then I heard it again. Not sure what to do, I went to write again. As I began to write the sentence, "Was that you, God?" my pen stopped working. I ran my pen in circles in the corner of the paper trying to get it to work. No ink would come out. My attention shifted to my pen, and frustration began to arise in me. *This is a new pen, and it's running dry the first time I use it?* As I fought with my pen I heard the word "Pray" for the third time. I immediately understood: my pen wasn't working, because I needed to pray.

I got down on my knees beside my bed and began to pray. I prayed for whatever came to mind. I prayed out loud because I was expecting something to happen. When I ran out of things to pray for I began declaring who God is. My mind started to get lost in the declarations. My voice and energy were rising. "God, You are good! You are perfect! You are my Savior! You are the Savior of the world! You are the King of Kings! You are high and lifted up! You are the Creator!" As I got lost in my declarations I felt the Spirit bubble up inside of me and each declaration seemed to come with more authority.

Then, the most exciting thing happened. I was declaring who God was with authority and suddenly realized I wasn't speaking English. I didn't know exactly when it happened, but I was no longer speaking English. In my mind I would say, "You are Lord of Lords," but the words I heard coming out of my mouth were not English. This was the most exciting thing that had ever happened to me; the Holy Spirit was literally flowing through me! I was so excited and I let it flow. I wasn't going to stop this powerful, transformational experience. Losing track of time I went on praying and declaring for quite a while. Who knows how long I was praying for. I kept going until it felt like it was done.

When I had finished I couldn't wait to journal about it. I picked up that pen, the same one that previously stopped working, and began to journal about my experience. It was no surprise to me when the pen worked perfectly fine just like a new pen should. This experience changed my life. I had never felt so fulfilled. I felt empowered by the living God Himself and encouraged; I finally understood this was where I belonged, with my God, and God had chosen and created me for a powerful purpose here on earth. I was sold out; I wanted to live with God, commune with God and walk with God all the days of my life. I couldn't wait to tell *everyone.*

Sharing my news with the YWAM base was a freeing experience. Everyone was excited and celebrated with me. My testimony was accepted, valued and celebrated which was so opposite from my life back home. It was a testimony I wanted everyone to hear. Even my mother. I shared my testimony with her over the phone. *There is no way she could deny this was God.* After excitedly sharing this with her there was no celebration on the other end of the phone. There wasn't really any response at all. *Did she hear me?* She assured me that she heard, there was just no response. I was too excited to let anything bring me down. I did not let her lack of a response affect me at all.

Months later, after my training at YWAM had ended, I was back living with my parents and seeking God for my next steps. One day my mother was really sick and did not get out of bed. I was in my room praying and felt the Lord prompt me to go and pray for her. I became very nervous. Anything having to do with prayer or talking about biblical or godly things was so awkward and rarely a good experience. I really didn't want to go. *God, I will pray for her healing from the comfort of my own room.* But the Lord wouldn't stop nudging my heart to go and ask her if I could pray for her. I didn't want to, but then I had the thought, *what if I am disobedient and Mom doesn't get well?* I couldn't live with that. "Okay, God, I will do it. Please go with me."

I really needed His encouragement, feeling like I was walking into the lion's den. It really shouldn't have been that hard, but it was.

I walked up to my mother's side. She opened her eyes and looked at me. I took a deep breath and went for it. "Can I pray for you?" There, I said it. It was out. I couldn't take it back now. My mother looked a little confused, but replied, "Okay."

Just before I began to pray I felt like God told me to lay my hands on her. I obediently asked her if I could lay hands on her. She agreed. I started to feel at peace more. This was going well, and I started to have hope that maybe something would break in the spiritual realm and my mother and I would begin to have a healthy relationship. Hope was rising within as I began to pray for the Lord to heal my mother and for the sickness to leave her body completely. When I had finished praying I felt another nudge. *Ask her if you can pray in the Spirit.* I immediately became sweaty; my heart rate rose and I became nervous all over again. I sensed that this wasn't going to end well, but I also felt I needed to be obedient. I didn't understand why the Lord wanted me to do this, but I had to trust there was a reason; a reason that would ultimately glorify His name. Remembering the God I served, I ask my mother if I could pray in the Spirit.

My mother seemed to become instantly angry. Her eyes narrowed as she stared at me with disapproval. Her entire countenance changed like I poked a demon that was influencing her and woke it up. I am absolutely not calling my mother a demon. She is a beautiful creation created by God for a powerful purpose, but I do believe we can all be influenced by demonic beings at times. This was one of those times. This was and is definitely not her true self, the powerful person she is designed to be. Whatever was influencing her in this moment was angry. My mother sternly responded with, "I never want to hear you praying in the Spirit in this house." "Okay," I answered. I got up and returned to my room.

In that moment I was, once again, hurt and confused. I was silenced and was being forced to put the shackles of limits back on. I didn't know what to do, but I was confident that I had been obedient and had to trust the Lord with what He wanted to do with the situation. The most difficult thing for me in that moment was not allowing a seed of bitterness to take root in my heart. I had to trust God and leave my mother in His hands.

More than 20 years later as I reflect on this memory I am not angry or bitter. I am filled with compassion for my mother. She honestly didn't know what she was doing. The enemy knows that I have a voice called to speak truth and draw others closer to God. The enemy was doing what he could to stop my voice, to put a muzzle on me. I now see the finger prints of the enemy all over my mother and I's relationship, sending his fiery arrows to shut me down in shame, believing I am worth nothing, fearing people's views about me and feeling that no one wants to hear me. Where I should have been celebrated I was silenced.

Praise the Lord for spiritual armor (Ephesians 6:10-19). I began to recite this verse daily and went through the motions of putting on this armor. I have learned to make the Lord's voice louder than the enemy's. I have prayed and asked for clarity and discernment for my painful memories, for current ones and future experiences. Taking responsibility for my own walk with the Lord, I am rebuking the witchcraft that was done to me unconsciously by my mother, such as word curses, false judgments, lies said about me, manipulation, and using her position to disempower me.

I forgive my mother 100%. I love her and pray that she will have her own powerful encounter with the Living God, an undeniable experience to cause those demonic influences to flee. Her own purpose and true identity is so much greater than she ever realized. And remember the gel pens she gave me in the care package? They are a significant part of my testimony. I believe God used those pens that came specifically from her for a reason. This testimony is not finished yet. My mother still has a part that has yet to come to pass.

Confused To Confident

Confidence is believing in ourselves. Confidence is not allowing circumstances, events or other people to change what we know to be true about ourselves. It is difficult to find self-confidence when it feels like the people we care most about express no confidence in us. When we are not fully accepted in our families, communities and church we wander down lonely paths that feed our confusion. This story is not unique to me. Many of us have traveled lonely roads trying to find a community who gives us permission to be ourselves. We were sent on these paths by the lies of the enemy through our loved ones. We will not find who we are or where we belong on these false paths.

The voice of the Lord is calling us off of these paths and back to Himself. He feels our pain, confusion and desperation. He is calling us to turn around and turn to Him. Our identity and our confidence is found in Him. And there is good news! We do not have to travel back the entire distance we have wandered. If we just turn around and start heading toward Him He will meet us where we are.

We never fit into the boxes our parents, teachers or churches tried to shove us into because we weren't supposed to fit. We have been created for a powerful purpose; a purpose that those functioning outside of the Holy Spirit do not see and cannot understand. Those who have bought into the lie that God only moves in certain already known ways don't understand. People who only work and move within a man-made system or institution don't understand. Most of the world does not understand who we are and what we were made for. We are unique. We have a call that no one else has had before. People cannot give us our identity, only God our Creator can. Let's take back what was stolen, find our confidence in our Creator, understand that we do not need human validation for our calling and live out God's original intent. God's original intent has been hidden from us, and we are called to unearth it and live it out...even in a world that doesn't get it.

It is not my mother's fault that she didn't accept me, validate my calling, understand my giftings or see the powerful purpose I was designed for. She is a product of a system that was conditioned to perform and keep to a specific way of doing things. Even though I did not receive from her what I felt I needed as a child all that time is not lost. God will use it all to glorify His name. There is purpose in the pressing and the pain I endured. Like Joseph who was sold into slavery by his own brothers may not have understood why God placed him in a family who hated him, there was purpose in all his pain and suffering. Every skill learned, every moment he chose to serve God rather than man or himself was later used to position Joseph to save the very family that sold him.

I do not know the end of my story, but I do know that God did not make a mistake giving me the mother I had. I am blessed for the lessons I learned, the pain I went through and all the hard, pressing, lonely wandering. He is turning it into a powerful anointing to break free from not only the bondages of an emotionally abusive mother, but also all bondages the enemy has had God's people trapped in. I trust the Lord will use this all to gain glory for His name, advance His Kingdom and to set people free from the clutches of the enemy, even my own family. I am declaring it! I can have confidence in who I am, I can trust what He asks me to do because I know He sees the greater picture. It will blow our minds when we see it. God is working, and I know He is working in my mother.

Rulers And Dominion Takers

We are called to return to, live out and demonstrate for a hurting world our original design. We were never made to be muzzled we were made to be heard. We were never made to live in the box of another's expectation or idea of who we should be. We were made to run and soar without limits. We were not created to live the victim's life. We were made to be rulers and to reign a dominion. We were made to be confident in who we are in God, not in who the world or any person says we are. God made us with an original design and that design was not meant to be jailed. To discover what our original intent is, we need to go back to the beginning, back to Genesis.

"Then God said, 'Let Us (Father, Son, Holy Spirit) make man in Our image, according to Our likeness [not physical, but a spiritual personality and moral likeness]; and let them have complete authority over the fish of the sea, the birds of the air, the cattle, and over the entire earth, and over everything that creeps *and* crawls on the earth.' So God created man in His own image, in the image *and* likeness of God He created him; male and female He created them. And God blessed them [granting them certain authority] and said to them, 'Be fruitful, multiply, and fill the earth, and subjugate it [putting it under your power]; and rule over (dominate) the fish of the sea, the birds of the air, and every living thing that moves upon the earth.'" Genesis 1:26-28 (AMP)

We see God's original intent for us in the first chapter of the Bible. The first part that stands out is, "let them have complete authority." WOW! I repeat, the Word of God says we were designed to have **complete authority**. That is a lot of power. We were originally designed to have and exercise authority, power and rulership. Over what exactly? It says, "over the fish of the sea, the birds of the air, the cattle, and over the entire earth, and over everything that creeps *and* crawls on the earth." That is a long, extensive list. However, what I notice is we have authority over every living thing on earth except another human being. Humans are not listed to be our subjects. I find that not only interesting but very informative.

We have been broken, frustrated, angry and bitter over a heartbreaking relationship with our mothers, and understandably so. Her emotional abuse was a way of controlling who we were and what we did and keeping us in bondage. Our feeling toward her behavior was instinctive. This mother/daughter relationship wasn't natural and was contrary to the Word of God. Human beings were not originally made to control other human beings.

In the same passage our original intent is reinstated: "Be fruitful, multiply, and fill the earth, and subjugate it [putting it under your power]; and rule over (dominate) the fish of the sea, the birds of the air, and every living thing that moves upon the earth." Notice the words *power*, *rule* and *dominate*. Again we see the list of living creatures we are to rule and dominate. Humans are not on that list. We naturally want to have power, which is evident everywhere with all the superhero movies, books, video games, board and card games, sports, politics, etc.

We naturally want to rule, which we can see in man's desire for successful careers and ownership of land, houses, cars and other material possessions. We naturally want to dominate. I am reminded of the children's game *king of the hill.* I used to play this as a child when the snowplows made giant piles of snow when clearing the school parking lot. With this giant snow pile we excitedly played this popular children's game. The point of the game was to push everyone else off of the top of snow hill and be the last one standing at the top. It was fun as long as the snow was soft and not hard and icy. This game demonstrates domination as a natural innate desire of human beings.

Even though this dominion, power and authority are an innate, natural part of our core being the problem is we have been striving to dominate and rule over the wrong things. This is where we see the breakdown of relationships. The role of a parent, as we saw through the demonstration of a loving Father in Proverbs, is to lead and guide their children. Yes, to correct, rebuke and teach them, to teach them to connect with the heart of the Father, train them to rule their God-given dominion, and glorify their God. It is not God's will for mothers to control their children.

We are designed to be dominion-takers. In the New King James translation it reads, "let them have dominion" God is our Creator and He is our King. He is not just any King, He is the Most High King of Kings (1 Tim. 6:15, Rev. 1:5, Rev. 17:14, Rev. 19:16). So when God speaks, His Word is law. Even though I am Canadian I am living in the United States. In this country we do not live under a sovereignty. Canada does have a queen, but we do not function under a sovereignty either. In God's Kingdom He is sovereign, so it can be difficult for us to wrap our minds around the significance of a king's word. However, let us submit to the Holy Spirit and allow Him to guide us to understand the laws of the spirit realm since we have not learned it in the physical realm.

In the book of Esther it is written, "Whatever is written in the King's name and sealed with the King's signet ring, no one can revoke" (Esther 8:8 NKJV). In Esther's time the destruction of God's people was already made into law, and the only way to save God's people was to make a new law (since the other one could not be revoked). In the same way, God's command was for the human race to rule and reign in their dominions. The devil stole our dominion by deceiving Eve in the Garden of Eden. When Jesus died on the cross He got the dominion back. Now through Christ we have dominion again.

Even though that's a spirit-realm truth the devil begins to lie to us, I believe, beginning in the womb. He has tricked us into thinking we are not worthy, not powerful, not favorable, etc. He tricked us into thinking we are less than who we are. If the devil can keep us from discovering our true identity as daughters of the Most High King, citizens of the heavenly Kingdom and servants of the Almighty God, he is able to keep us in bondage, and specifically, according to the purpose of this book, to a narcissistic, emotionally abusive mother.

"God saw everything that He had made, and behold, it was very good *and* He validated it completely. And there was evening and there was morning, a sixth day." Genesis 1:31 (AMP)

When our Creator finished making the human being He declared all that He had made *very good*. The definition of good is, "Of high quality; excellent" (dictionary.com). Synonyms of good include: excellent, exceptional, valuable, favorable, wonderful, pleasing and worthy (thesaurus.com). In this we see more of who we were made to be. God called the human *very good*. Our original intent was to be *very good*. If we switch the word *good* for some of its synonyms we get a deeper understand of who we were at creation. God called us excellent, exceptional, valuable, favorable, wonderful, pleasing, and worthy. It is no wonder the enemy has attacked us with lies that literally counter what God says.

Satan works hard making sure the truth about who we are is hidden from us. Not only does he hide it, he plays our emotions and uses those closest to us make us feel the opposite of the truth. Hence we have the inner critic, emotional tugs of war and internal struggles. It is a battle between the innate truth of who we are and our emotions of how *we feel* we are.

Again, I repeat, our feelings may be real but they are not always the truth. It is essential to know the Word of God for checking our feelings. If our feelings are contrary to the Word we need to rebuke those feelings and speak truth over ourselves. God said we are *good*; Satan makes us feel no good. God said we are valuable; Satan makes us feel devalued. God said we are favorable; Satan makes us feel like we have no favor anywhere. God says we are pleasing, Satan makes us feel like we don't please anyone and nobody likes or cares for us. God says we are worthy, Satan makes us feel worthless. The accuser's strategies have remained the same throughout history. Familiarize yourself with these strategies, and fight back with the Word of God, with truth.

I Am A Masterpiece

God made us in the likeness of Himself (Gen. 1:27). We are a beautiful piece of art created by God who used Himself as the model. We were not incomplete. We were not broken. We were not flawed. For an artist to declare a piece of their own work very good the art is in its complete form, fulfilled to the desire of the artist's heart and to its fullest intent. With God Himself as the model this art, the original human, was perfect.

"You, therefore, will be perfect [growing into spiritual maturity both in mind and character, actively integrating godly values into your daily life], as your heavenly Father is perfect."
Matthew 5:48 (AMP)

At creation we were made perfectly and completely. We were made whole and intended to have a WHOLE life: emotionally, spiritually, mentally, financially, in health, and in relationships with both people and God! That whole life was stolen at the fall of man, but Jesus bought us back with His blood on Calvary's cross. God's original intent is *still* His intent for us today. His plan has not changed. We are made to be completely whole and perfect.

In the hands of the devil we were misused, broken, scratched up, bruised, and became dirty. Our Heavenly Father, our Creator, our Savior, has redeemed us. Since being bought back we have been in the process of being cleaned up, glued back together, scrubbed, sewn, and painted to return us back to our original intent. We didn't see what we looked like at the beginning; therefore, we need to trust our Father's ways as He works on us. He knows who we are, what we are to look like and how we are to think and act.

"Therefore if anyone is in Christ [that is, grafted in, joined to Him by faith in Him as Savior], *he is* a **new** creature [reborn and renewed by the Holy Spirit]; the old things [the previous moral and spiritual condition] have passed away. Behold, **new** things have come [because spiritual awakening brings a **new** life]."
2 Corinthians 5:17 (AMP)

In Christ we are new and being made new. For the rest of our lives here on earth we will be learning to be the new creation – our original intent. There are levels of growth the Lord will take us through as we are obedient and allow Him to work on and through us. This is beautiful. The more we engage in our own transformation and humbly yield to the work of the Holy Spirit there will be upgrades of who Jesus is to us.

For me, at first He was just a person who saved me from my sins and the consequence of hell. Then, He became a friend who comforted me when I was down and lonely and stayed by my side as I navigated through unknown territory and life experiences. Later He became a lover who loved me deeply and unconditionally. The more I engage in this relationship the depth and layers of His love continue to be revealed. At every level there is a new understanding of His majesty bringing me in awe of Him again. He is a Father who truly never stops fighting for His children.

The more we grow as a new creation and return to who we were meant to be the more we want to grow. As much as it hurts, the pain and discomfort of the cleansing, washing and fixing actually becomes exciting because we understand this is for our own good. It is part of the process of returning to our original design and becoming who we were meant to be. There is something excellent on the other side that blesses us and takes us deeper and higher at the same time. We always enter new levels of freedom and with each level become passionate about seeing others be set free as well. Let us remain excited for our growth.

Confident Is Who I Am

Let us have confidence in who God created us to be. We are powerful. We are rulers. We are problem solvers. We are called to bring light and life into a dark world saturated in a death culture. We are not the problem even though our mothers made us feel like we were. We are co-creators with our Creator called to create new things, carve new paths and be agents of change. It is time to live a new way, God's way, the way we are designed to live, our original intent. We are part of a movement calling people back to the heart of the Father.

Jesus Himself came to show us a new way of living: the Kingdom way of living. To enter this Kingdom we need to repent from our sin, wrong thinking, inaccurate mindsets, conforming to man's systems, putting God in a box by giving Him our limits, putting ourselves in a box by limiting what we can and cannot do, etc. We need to repent from partnering with lies of the enemy and allowing ourselves to be used as agents of bondage. Jesus called us to repent so that we can enter into the Kingdom of God, the Kingdom of true freedom, the Kingdom of wholeness and healing. We are called to be the Kingdom here on earth and be breakers of tradition (the old system of doing things). It is time to usher in God's way of doing things and break free from man's way.

The world desperately needs what we have. It is time for us to release what God has put inside of us. The power, the strength, the creativity, the problem-solving, it has been there the whole time. We were created with it inside of us; it has just been buried by so much junk from the world, but it is there. It is time to throw off the labels the world has stuck on us and to declare out loud who God says we are.

Make A Self-Declaration

Say these out loud. Say them like you mean it, powerfully and with purpose. Say it until you believe it! These statements are true because they are taken from the Word of God.

> I am the salt of the earth - Matthew 5
> I am the light of the world - Matthew 5:14
> I am the head and not the tail - Deut. 28:13
> I am above and not beneath - Deut. 28:13
> I am more than a conqueror - Romans 8:37
> I am an overcomer - 1 John 5:4
> I am free - Luke 4:18
> I am an approved worker for God - 2 Timothy 2:15
> I am a king (queen) and a priest of the Most High - Rev. 1:6
> I am an heir to the King - Romans 8:17
> I am a friend of God - John 15:15

I am His beloved - Psalm 127:2
I am blessed - Psalm 112:1
I am the joy set before Him - Hebrews 12:2
I am anointed - 2 Cor. 1:21
I am made in the image of God - Genesis 1:27
I am exquisitely fashioned - Job 10:8
I am a child of God - Deut. 14:1
I am a temple - 1 Cor. 3:16
I am crucified with Christ - Gal. 2:20
I am redeemed - Gal. 3:13
I am a royal priest - 1 Peter 2:10
I am a living stone - 1 Peter 2:4
I am a holy nation - 1 Peter 2:9
I am an heir of God - Romans 8:17
I am a branch connected to the vine - John 15:5
I am His disciple - John 8:31
I am His body - Romans 12:5
I am a daughter of the Great I AM - Romans 8:16-17
I am being transformed into the image of God - 1 Cor. 3:17-18,
Phil. 3:20-21, Romans 8:28-29, Romans 12:1-2

Unboxed Prayer

Father in Heaven,

Thank you for revealing to me who I am to You. Thank you for taking away the things that led me to believe a false identity. I give You permission to continue to reveal the high places in my life and everything I have held on to or have attached my identity to that is false and damaging. Remove everything that keeps me from You. I want to be fully committed to You and fully confident in who I am in You. As a child I trusted in my mother which led me to false beliefs about myself. Today I declare I put my trust in You. My trust is no longer in any human being. My desire is for my trust to be completely in You. I put my trust in every word that comes from Your mouth. I rebuke every word from any source that has been spoken over me and does not line up with Your Word. Fill me up completely with Your Spirit. Fill up every place in my heart, the open spaces, the storage spaces, the little corner spaces. I want to be completely filled with You and never tempted to gratify my flesh. Bring healing in my life where healing feels impossible. I praise You, Lord, for the work You have done in my heart and in my life. Never stop working on me. I want to be an effective vessel for Your Kingdom.

All the power and all the glory is Yours, AMEN!

ELEVEN

Renewed Mind, My Transformation

"Mom, Mom!" I called out as I walked into the house. There was no answer, so I kept calling her name, "Mom! Mom!" Still nothing. I went upstairs calling, "Mom! Mom!" I was confused. *Where could she be?*

"Mom?" I called out one more time.

"She's in Edmonton," my brother called back. I walked to the room where his voice came from. When I finally had eyes on my brother I asked,

"Where is Mom?"

"She went to Edmonton. She is not here."

"What? When will she be back?" I was so confused and hurt at the same time. It was Friday afternoon, and I had a question I wanted to ask her and she wasn't home, she wasn't in the same city, she wasn't even in the same province, and I had no idea. No heads up. Nothing.

"I don't know, I think Monday," my brother replied.

"How do you know she went to Edmonton?"

"She told me," he answered.

As I walked away I was so hurt I wanted to cry. My mother took a weekend trip to Edmonton, a city in another province and never told me, but she told my brother. When my father returned home from work that night I told my dad about my mother not telling me she was leaving for the weekend, and he brushed it off as if it were no big deal. He knew she was going and didn't think to mention it to me either. He had no reason why.

I went that whole weekend consumed by mixed emotions,

215

swinging back and forth between anger and hurt. Then, at the same time I felt completely alone with no one to talk to about what I was going through emotionally. I had to hide my emotions around my father and brother or else they accused me of being too sensitive. "Lighten up," or "Why do you have to make such a big deal out of everything?" they would say. So I would bottle it inside, doing my best to "not make a big deal" out of anything.

On Monday after my mother returned home I decided I would confront her about how her lack of communication made me feel. It wasn't easy. I had thought about it all weekend, but I felt like it had to be done. I remember sitting on the stairs, anxiety raging through my body, my hands becoming clammy and my heart racing while I gave myself a pre-confrontation pep talk. The spirit of fear was hugging me tight as I rose from those stairs, determined not to back down. She needed to know how I felt. I just wished talking to my mother wasn't so difficult.

"Mom," I managed to say, hoping she wouldn't notice me trembling.

"Yes," she answered

"You know, you going to Edmonton for the weekend without telling me really hurt," I blurted it out, immediately questioning if I said the wrong thing.

My mother's eyes narrowed, her glare sliced through me like a hot knife in butter, feeding the guilt, shame and rejection in the center of my heart and causing it to grow. "I don't have to tell you anything."

Her harsh words would crush me, forcing me into submission once again to the lie that I was unworthy, and I sunk deeper into my insecurity.

My emotional need to feel valued was not met by my mother. Hiding things and information from me that I needed to know created fear and insecurity in me as a child, teenager and young adult. My mother would argue that I didn't need to know, but I actually did to feel emotionally safe, secure and valued. As I reflect on this memory, I ask Jesus, "Where were You in that moment? Where were You when I was being crushed by my mother's pain? Why wasn't my courage to confront her honored? Where were You?"

In reply, the Lord has given me a picture of that moment. He took me back to the bottom of the stairs by the garage door where this painful memory took place. And for the first time I saw Jesus there. He was there trying to reach out to me, but I was clinging on to fear. Then, I see Him standing behind my mother, looking lovingly at me, yet sad at the same time. His arms spread open wide, ready to embrace His hurting child, but as the event comes to a close I rush past Him, choosing to run with anger instead. I then see Jesus put His arm on my mother's shoulder. Jesus was reaching out, wanting to take her pain, but she doesn't know He is there. She doesn't realize the weight she is carrying doesn't have to be carried any more. The next image I see of my mother is startling; she is rugged stone from the middle of her abdomen down to her toes. She turns to leave the house, moving slowly as she shifts and moves her rock body. I had no idea my mother had been carrying around so much weight.

The Lord revealed to me every harsh word, every cut down, every control mechanism she used against me was her way of subconsciously transferring the weight of her own pain over to me. She has been trying to ease her own pain, relieve some of her own emotional weight, by heaping it onto me. Why me and not my brother or sister? It is because I am the one who carries a similar, powerful calling; a calling she has been convinced doesn't exist. I am the one who is most like her. I am the free-spirited, determined, strong and resilient one like her. She has been conditioned to follow tradition and believes that is what is best for me too, but unlike her, the wildness that flows in my veins will not allow me to be content in a system run by tradition. I had to break free.

Unknown to my mother the enemy has been using her to tame the wildness in me. What she doesn't understand is the wildness that runs through my veins is a new breed of wild, one that cannot be tamed. It is a unique strain of wild God has created for the times we are living in now. And I sense that my mother carries the weight of failure, feeling that she has failed in her inability to tame me.

It wasn't her fault. I cannot be tamed. I may have been muzzled for a time and slowed down and distracted by the weight of my own emotional pain, but when I realized I loved myself enough to fight for me I made the choice to run after healing and find the abundant joy-filled life I felt so strongly was mine. Where can I find and learn to fully embrace the wild and free real me? From the one who made me, the one and only Creator God. I cannot change my mother or our past, but I can love myself enough to change me, the way I think, the way I act and change the direction I go. The anger I once had toward my mother is a choice, and I choose to give it to God.

When I made this choice I knelt down on the floor with my arms stretched out in front of me as a symbol of giving up the anger I held toward my mother for causing me such emotional pain. I was giving it to God. To live the wild and free life I was called to live I couldn't carry around the weight of anger. With my hands stretched out and the anger taken away I asked God to replace the anger with something else. Immediately the word *compassion* came to mind, and I knew God was giving me compassion for my mother to replace the anger I once had.

I was renewing my mind; I was changing the way I thought about my mother. Now when I think of her and the pain she carries around like rocks, compassion floods me, and I pray she will have such a mighty encounter with the Living God that she will give up those rocks and embrace her true, free, passionate self.

A Renewed Mind

Simply put, a renewed mind is choosing to interpret life through a different set of lenses than we previously did. I once interpreted my identity and purpose through the actions and words of others. Also when my needs, specifically my emotional needs, were not being met I looked at others around me. *Oh, I see how they're getting their needs*

218

met, so I'll try that too. I behaved in ways I shouldn't have to meet needs of acceptance and feelings of worthiness. I ran after worldly forms of success hoping to find some sort of fulfillment.

I was viewing life through the wrong set of lenses. Paul in the Bible says this about having a renewed mind:

"Do not conform to the pattern of this world, but be transformed by the renewing of your mind. Then you will be able to test and approve what God's will is—his good, pleasing and perfect will."
Romans 12:2 (NIV)

Having a renewed mind is not just the avoidance of certain external behaviors. A person can make an entire religion out of avoiding certain external behaviors but be completely bitter and miserable on the inside. That's not real freedom. Actually, that is another form of bondage, and Jesus came to set us free from all bondage. Having a renewed mind is not just acting differently, it is thinking differently and seeing life differently, and as a result behaving differently.

For me, renewing my mind was changing what I put into it. I changed what I read, what I watched, who I listened to and who I followed. Specifically, I stopped looking at what other people were doing and starting asking the Father what He wanted me to do. I started getting counsel from wise people who loved the Lord and were filled with the Holy Spirit. I allowed my eyes to be opened to see the systems, boxes, labels and traditions that I didn't want to follow. I chose not to turn a blind eye to programs that were sucking the life out of me. I chose not to comply to the world for the sake of "keeping the peace" or "fitting in."

I chose to see life through the eyes of my Creator and the way I was designed to live. Despite how my mother made me feel I had a heavenly design. I no longer wanted to be a caterpillar, but a gorgeous, colorful, free butterfly. The only way to make this massive transformation is to have a renewed mind.

Why Should We Renew The Mind?

We can be blinded by lies we partnered with. Renewing our minds with the Word of God clears our vision of our self, life around us and our place in it all. Renewing our mind gives us clarity of direction for our lives and clarity of thought for life's situations. Renewing our mind gives us a new perspective on what is important in life. Things we previously tolerated we no longer have grace for. Renewing our mind shifts the way we spend our time, creating a desire to use time more wisely and effectively. Renewing our mind may tear us away from old ways of doing things as the Lord leads us to the new.

In the process of the tearing away we may notice some people getting offended, yet we are not. We simply find ourselves extending grace in areas we once became defensive. Many things will just not matter anymore because we want the new. Without a renewed mind we may find ourselves running on empty with no hope of refueling. Having a renewed mind through Christ provides refreshment and endless opportunities for filling up. We were not designed to be running on empty. We need to see ourselves how Jesus sees us: highly valued and highly favored.

In the past what I believed in my mind was not always what I believed in my heart. There was a disconnect. God wants unity between heart and mind. Renewing our mind through the Word of God and following the guidance of the Holy Spirit brings that desired peace and unity between the heart and the mind. We are worth it. This is our original design: to have our heart, soul and mind unified. When there is emotional pain, which is caused my unmet needs, our connection with God needs to be healed.

If we do not get our needs met in Him we will get our needs met in unhealthy ways, which severs our connection with God our Creator. A fish can only live so long out of the water. A flower begins to die when cut from its roots, and a branch will no longer produce beautiful leaves and flowers apart from the tree. We need to have a renewed mind to remain in connection with our Creator and be transformed into our full purpose.

Let me share one more thing about renewing our minds. Why should we renew our mind with God's Word and the Holy Spirit? Because God always trades up. If you remember, I traded my anger for compassion, right? Compassion is so much lighter to carry around! And compassion and joy are very complimentary to each other. Where anger suppressed my joy, compassion ushers it out of me.

I remember a time when my heart was so full of compassion for an elderly couple who lost everything in a tornado. I spent days helping with debris removal on their property, and the joy kept bubbling out of me the entire time I was working. The joy was energizing me, and I never felt tired even though I was working long hours in the hot sun. When others were taking breaks I was singing and bouncing around, hauling debris to the curb of the street. I really was bouncing. Other volunteers told me that I made them smile because it looked like I was bouncing around the yard effortlessly picking up all the debris. The compassion ushered the joy out, and I was blessed to help out this amazing elderly couple who since then have been blessed with a new home.

God is so good. His plans for us are greater than we can imagine. When we give up the hurt, pain, anger and bitterness and whatever else we have been carrying around God always trades up. We give Him the negative and He gives us a blessing. He wants us to have better lives, better experiences, better communities. We see how God trades up in Isaiah 61:3:

"...to bestow on them a crown of beauty instead of ashes, the oil of joy instead of mourning, and a garment of praise instead of a spirit of despair. They will be called oaks of righteousness, a planting of the LORD for the display of his splendor."

Renewing our minds is not about erasing our memories but

healing them and seeing Jesus in them. Also every single memory does not need to be healed in order to experience healing and freedom from them. We want to fill the spaces of our beings, our heart, soul and minds with the pleasure of our King and our Creator. With a renewed mind and a healed heart we can allow ourselves to feel celebrated, we can spread our wings, we can spread out, we can soar, we can run, we can dance. We are not *too much* if the people around us cannot handle us; they need to take it up with the Father in Heaven, because we are here to be all He created us to be, not who others want us to be.

What Will A Renewed Mind Look Like?

It is time to dance and praise the Lord! Tear off every label the world made you wear, put on those garments of praise and let the Lord put a ring on your finger and a royal robe on your shoulders! We are royalty; we are daughters of the King of Kings. May our ears be sharpened to the hear the voice of the Lord and may the words the world throws at us that are not in line with the Word of God fall to the ground and be trampled on. We will not be haunted or halted by perfectionism, but we will be full-time, passionate lovers of God who are not afraid of taking imperfect actions.

Our renewed minds can shake off the past like Lazarus taking off his grave clothes. The truth of God's Word renews our mind and peels off the layers of trauma, pain, religious abuse, emotional abuse, rejection, and bondage from the spirit of witchcraft. Fear of man will no longer keep us shackled. We will not tolerate the mundane life of routine and tradition. We will be free from mixing the world's way and God's way for the sake of balance and peace. We are only driven by the real deal, the purity of God's Word.

Let's take our renewed mind and healed heart to the world and be healers and restorers of hearts and God-given purposes. We will carry the heart of God to a world that is confused and lost. We will cut through the darkness with the Shekinah Glory of God as His torch bearers, bringing life to a world that has embraced a culture of death. We will uplift the image of God and watch idols crumble in our families, churches and communities. We will be a people of honor even though we have been repeatedly dishonored by those who do not understand who we are.

How Do I Renew My Mind?

One effective way to renew my mind is simply asking God questions, allowing Him to respond and then act on what He says. First, let us ask God this question: what am I believing about myself that isn't true? If new thoughts or things I haven't thought of in many years pop into my mind this is how I know God is talking to me.

After the Lord has revealed a lie that I am believing about myself I repent for partnering with the lie. If there are any emotions I have been carrying around with this lie, such as anger, bitterness, jealousy, disappointment, etc., this is where I give it to God. I will literally say, "Lord, take my ___ (name emotion) ___." Then, I ask, "What do You have for me in return?" This is where I will hear the Lord speak in my mind. I often hear another emotion that is one of the fruits of the Spirit or is associated with one (Galatians 5:22).

Then, I continue by asking God another question: "What lie am I believing about You?" I pause and wait for a response. Again, this response often comes in a form of an impression, a picture or a thought that just pops into my head. If the Lord reveals a lie I have been believing about Him I repent for believing it and ask Him to replace it lie with a truth about Him. I will allow the Lord to speak to me. Sometimes the Holy Spirit will lead me to the Bible where I will read scriptures about the truth of who God is that counter the lie I had been believing.

It is important to make these kinds of meetings with God a regular thing. We are human and will sometimes partner with a lie unknowingly, and we need to make sure we keep our hearts and minds in check and in line with the Word of God. There are many lies we have all believed over the course of our lives, in my experience God does not deal with all of them at once. That would be too much to handle. In my life the Lord has revealed one or two lies at a time and gives me time to clean my mind and heart of the lie and wash my mind with the truth of His Word.

Another way to renew my mind is what I surround myself with. For example, listening to worship music and to Holy Spirit-filled teachers who reveal the truth of God's Word. I also read the Bible daily and surround myself with a circle of friends who are lovers of Jesus, passionate about seeing His will fulfilled through me and keep me accountable and encourage my faith walk. I am careful with the movies I watch and what thoughts I think. Not everything that pops into my head is a thought I need to entertain. There are many garbage thoughts that come into my head that need to be dismissed immediately.

In the process of renewing my mind I have felt a pull in a new direction and my focus changes. Sometimes the tearing away of my old life has its painful moments, but the freedom I experience on the other side is worth it. I have definitely felt displaced and a little lost on a new path, in a new direction, in a new a place I have never been before and especially when I have never seen anyone in my family or community there before either.

I feel like the Lord has me forging a new path like a trailblazer, demonstrating the higher call God has for us all. There have been times I have felt alone on this journey because no one else sees life the way I do. Maybe I am looked at as a fool for not walking the well-worn path, but I dare to follow God to forge new ones. There is a burning desire in my heart to enter this new area with God and take the new spiritual office God has reserved for me. I believe God has a high call for each of us and a reserved spiritual office for us to operate out of. And when I say new, I mean *new*, never before occupied by another. This is why we need to have a renewed mind to protect ourselves from being offended when people do not understand the road we are traveling with God. It hasn't been traveled before; the world won't understand.

The good news is we are not alone. Although I felt alone when I walked away from the toxic relationship with my mother, the Lord led me to my tribe. I began to meet people in random ways; people who have the same wild blood running through their veins, who have been misunderstood by their communities, who have been running after complete healing, who will forge new trails that will advance the Kingdom of God, and draw others closer to Himself and glorify His name. It is all for the Kingdom. Everything we do is for the Kingdom, God's Kingdom, the Kingdom of Light, the Kingdom of Freedom.

In order to forge new trails our minds must be strong, rooted in truth and healthy. We can develop healthy thinking habits. Each person has the power to control their thoughts and change toxic thinking into healthy thinking. We have the power to change from feeling sorry for ourselves in our thoughts to having thoughts of gratitude. Stressful thoughts can be changed into excitement. It is limitless the things we can think, both positive and negative.

Our Creator is a limitless God, and in Him we are a part of a limitless Kingdom. In the past we have been conditioned to limit our thoughts about ourselves – who we are and what we can and cannot do. However, that conditioning is not true. We are limitless in our minds with our thoughts and our imagination. We can train our minds to have thoughts that lead us to success rather than entertaining thoughts of potential failure. Focusing on failure can cause us to not even try to go after the dreams of our hearts. Let us train ourselves to not limit our thoughts and imagination and to think positively and highly of who we are and our powerful purpose on this earth.

Unboxed Prayer

Father,

I am so excited to be chosen by You at this time. Thank you for my renewed mind. I love seeing the world through these new lenses. This is the way You have intended for me to see the world all along. Please continue to increase in me, expand my vision and grow me into my full purpose that I may experience the abundant life You have designed for me. May I step fully into the call You have on my life and see Your Kingdom come here on earth as it is in Heaven.

In the mighty name of Jesus, AMEN!

TWELVE

Unboxed, My Heart

I sat on the porch of a camp dining hall staring into the gorgeous blue eyes of a wonderful older woman. A friend of mine who had also grown up in a toxic environment encouraged me to talk to this wonderful woman about my relationship with my mom. My friend had recently met with her and had a life-altering experience of having her mother wounds healed. On my friend's recommendation, on this porch a piece of my heart healed in a way I didn't think possible.

After briefly sharing my story with this wise woman she gently took my hand into hers and looked deep into my eyes. As I stared back I saw so much love and compassion I could have gone swimming in it. I didn't know exactly what she was doing until she started to speak. This wonderful, Holy Spirit-filled woman was standing in the gap for my mother, speaking to me as if she *was* my mother. Holy Spirit flowed through her as she began apologizing for every short coming as a mother she had. She asked for forgiveness for every time she hurt me without realizing it, for it was never her intention. With deep sorrow coming out with every word this angel from the Lord said she was sorry for every time she caused me pain and suffering.

There was a point in her heart wrenching apology when I genuinely felt I was no longer staring into a stranger's eyes, but into the eyes of my mother herself. Her eyes genuinely looked like my mother's, and I began to cry. I had previously come to peace with the fact that I may never hear an apology, so I left the expectation at the feet of Jesus. I no longer longed for, hoped for or sought after my mother recognizing how terribly hurtful her actions were and offering an authentic apology. Jesus took it, and therefore it took me by surprise when He took what I gave up and gave it back to me. The Lord gave me the most authentic, heartfelt apology. He knew I needed to hear these words. He knew I needed to see the authenticity in my mother's eyes. He knew these words and these eyes would heal my heart in a way nothing else could.

Tears streamed down my face. Every word was like a soothing ointment on a wound accelerating its healing and reducing the potential visibility of a scar. When the words were done we sat for a few peaceful moments; I soaked in the sincerity I saw in her eyes. When I finally found my words I responded, "I forgive you." My words were pure and matched the authenticity of the words spoken to me. I meant them. I forgave my mother. Totally and completely. My heart filled with compassion as I understood in my heart how my mother truly didn't know what she did to me – the pain she caused or that she was cutting me down and trying to force me to be who I was not designed to be. I believe my mother sensed the power of my calling but didn't understand it and didn't know what to do with it so she did only what she knew. My mother did her best with what she knew.

Looking back on this moment I see Jesus hugging me. Not the sneaky from behind hug…the full-on Daddy bear hug from the front, pulling me in close and squeezing me the way a loving father does. His face is beaming like a proud Father, excited for His daughter who just accomplished something that took years of work. He understood the difficult road and the courage and bravery it took to release it completely and forgive the one human who meant the most to me throughout my childhood. My Heavenly Father, who understands completely, gave me a beautiful gift that day; He filled my heart and released me in a new way to pursue my calling with a fresh passion.

A Mother's Blessing

About a year after the beautiful gift of an authentic, sincere apology the Lord provided another wonderful, chain-breaking gift I didn't even know I needed: a mother's blessing. At this time I was part of a training team at a missions organization that hosts regular events designed to equip Kingdom saints for walking out their calling and being light in times of crisis. During one particular training event we had a team come in to train us on inner healing through prayer. We had many opportunities for practicing what we learned, and it was an honor to witness freedom from various heart wounds in many of the participants.

After a lesson on the necessity, significance and power of the verbal declarations and blessings the ministry leader had us participants find partners to immediately practice what we learned about standing in the gap for an individual to aid them in the healing of their heart. I was divinely paired with a woman who was old enough to be my mother; she was actually about ten years older than my mother, but she fit the mother role perfectly for me.

We began with prayer, making an authentic connection with God and allowing His Holy Spirit to guide the moment. The Lord revealed with a picture that I had a heart wound from the trauma of lack I had experienced from my mother. The picture the Lord showed me exposed how I wasn't the kind of child my mother was expecting. Due to my mother's expectations not being met I suffered the heart wound of rejection as a baby. My emotional needs were not met by her and my emotional pain was not validated by her. As a result, I lacked the support and empowerment from her to embrace my calling from the Lord.

This trauma of lack I felt had already been dealt with and healed, yet one thing was still missing. To affirm and bless what God had already done in my life on this magnificent healing journey I needed a blessing from my mother; I needed her to agree with and support what God was doing in my life. The blessing from a mother affirms, validates, heals and frees. This beautiful woman who was standing in the gap for my biological mother listened to me with attentiveness as I shared the picture God gave me about my trauma of lack from my mother. With love in her eyes this mother gently took my hand, looked me in the eyes and with complete genuineness, validated and affirmed me with a mother's blessing.

"Kari, I would like to stand in the gap as a mother and say that you are incredibly precious to me. I bless the day you were conceived. The angels rejoiced in the heavens as you were brought to life. I bless the day you were born; it was a beautiful day full of excitement, anticipation and celebration. You are a blessing to me, to your family, to your community and to the whole world. I want to affirm that you are beautiful, both inside and out. You are an attractive woman and you glow with the glory of God. I affirm your personality is wonderful and you are a delight to be around. You radiate joy everywhere you go. You are uniquely creative. There is no one else like you. Without you this world would be lacking. You have a powerful purpose that no one else can fulfill, and I bless all that God in doing in your life both now and in the future. As a mother I am very proud of you, and I call you to embrace and step into everything God designed you for. I bless with all my heart, every expression of who you are. "

Reading this blessing again I have chills running up and down my spine. I feel honored, I feel heard, I feel seen, I feel valued, I feel empowered, and I feel chosen. I feel like a whole person lacking nothing. I feel superhuman. With God's hand in mine and my mother's blessing nothing can stop what the Lord has for me. I can confidently say I have a purpose and I need to fulfill it. I want to fulfill it. I am excited to fulfill it.

I Am Celebrated

Discovering my true identity, choosing to fully embrace it and determined to live my life to the fullest, I have come to realize the significance of forming an inner circle of Kingdom-minded warrior friends who celebrate me, not tolerate me. Gone are the days where I feel I need to put up with being tolerated by people. If I am being tolerated and not celebrated I have permission to politely say goodbye and move on. I am free to pick my people. My mother may not have seen how amazingly I was created, but I now know and understand that she senses it. It is an undeniable sense, and I am so thankful the Lord revealed this truth to me.

My inner circle of people is so important to me. My inner circle is filled with people who have such high respect for Jesus. They do not only recognize my significance in the Kingdom, but they love, edify, up lift, guide, train, correct, equip, and pray for me to live out my God-ordained purpose.

Remember the powerful scripture about Jehu in 2 Kings 9? Jehu's fellow army officers spoke the Word of the Lord back to Jehu, encouraging him in his purpose, and as a result Jehu was able to lead an army and wipe out the most wicked leaders the world had ever seen. This is like my circle; we ride together to conquer the world.

Also, I have learned to remain open to the Lord when He brings people to me who need this kind of community. Remember, we are not alone in breaking free from the bondages of an emotionally abusive mother. As we walk out our freedom others who are suffering from what we just received freedom from will be drawn to us. I choose to be completely transparent. I choose to love and counsel people through my healing and not my pain.

This book has been my story of healing and how it has impacted me. Each of us has our own story that needs to be told. Someone somewhere needs to hear our story! We must not be silent or shy about sharing our healing journeys because it can be used by God to heal someone else. It could bring a sense of belonging, give permission to feel celebrated and the courage to fight for freedom.

I Won't Waste My Life

As much as my heart longs for a healthy relationship with my mother, I chose to not wait around for it. This would be wasting the beautiful life God has for me. I am made for an abundant, joy-filled life. Waiting around for someone else is not living, it is existing. I have a higher calling, so I chose to give my mother completely to the Lord. She is not my problem, and I am not hers. My mother belongs to the Lord, and I need to trust in Him to work on her in His timing. The only thing I can do is to release her to the Lord and pray.

When I pray for her I pray she will have an amazing encounter with the Lord. I pray she will receive life-transforming revelations from the Lord. I pray she feels deeply loved by her Heavenly Father. I pray for her healing. I pray she will get delivered from every bondage she is living under and experience true freedom. I pray she will be filled with an abundance of joy like she has never known before.

Proud To Be Me

I am a beautiful masterpiece designed by the greatest artist of all time who was never meant to be hidden. My Heavenly Father is proud of who I am, and I am too. This past year I lost count of how many people approached me and said, "I feel like the Lord wants you to know that He is proud of you." The first time it happened I didn't take the word seriously (maybe because I didn't quite believe it). By the time the third person said it though I started to take notice. These people didn't know each other, and each word was given at a different random time. The fourth and fifth time I knew, without a doubt, God was speaking to me. Then, I realized how hard I'd been on myself for every imperfect step I made in the direction God was leading me. I had to stop counting myself out and thinking I was failing; the imperfect steps in the direction God was leading was exactly what I was supposed to be doing.

I needed to hear and believe what God was saying: He was proud of me, and I should be too. To help this sink into my spirit I said this out loud, "I am proud of who God made me to be." It felt good to say it. Writing this I am reminding myself to make this a habit. *Note to self: tell myself that I am worth being proud of.*

My mother made me feel ashamed of who I was, and as a result I boxed myself up and stuffed myself down into the storage places of my heart. Trying to be who I thought my mother wanted me to be was exhausting, frustrating and never worked. This strategy for living life, trying to live to please another human being, was a failure. I had to tear that plan up and throw it in the garbage. I am no longer in this bondage. God is proud of me, His daughter! God made me AWESOME! God made me His masterpiece, a work of outstanding artistry! I am proud to be me!

God Dreams

I am called to be fully alive without feeling like I have to shrink back. The stored-up dreams in my heart are there for a reason. They are there to make impact for the Kingdom of God; they are there to bring Heaven on earth and to set captives free. The dreams in my heart are there for solving problems I am designed to solve.

And guess what? My mother doesn't have to support, validate or even like my dreams. My dreams are not designed for her. God put them in my heart for Him, and He has full intentions of seeing those dreams come to pass. I believe my mother can benefit from the God dreams in my heart coming to pass, but they are ultimately there to glorify God. My dreams are uniquely designed to draw others closer to God and advance His Kingdom in a way only I can. I must always remember to seek first His Kingdom, His heart, invest in my relationship with my Creator and trust Him to bring my dreams into a reality. The same goes for you.

Not only has God put dreams in our hearts, I also believe there is a movement inside waiting for the right moment to burst forth from us. God's heart will be revealed through these movements, and as imperfect and unpolished as it may be, God will be in it. There is a movement in you! There is an anointing pouring out for fresh movements across the globe, and one of my dreams is to be in the middle of a great movement of seeing heart wounds healed, dormant dreams waking up, supernatural strategies exploding, creativity taking new heights, and waves of God-fearing, Kingdom-minded men and women locking arms in harmony, each confident in their own part in advancing God's Kingdom here on earth. I have a dream where God's people are no longer trying to one up each other, competing for higher positions in the man-made, society hierarchy, but rather support and complement each other. What is the big God dream in your heart?

The movement in our hearts will converge with each others' like streams converging on their way to the ocean. Through these movements God's Spirit will be poured out and flood the least expected places to bring healing, freedom and truth. Eyes will be opened and deception exposed, and the most surprising people, to the religious crowds, will turn their hearts to their Heavenly Father. As a result, fathers' and mothers' hearts will be turned to their children and repentance will come in massive waves. Emotional wounds will be healed, hearts will be awakened and eyes will be opened for the first time to their involvement in a culture of death. The mass abandoning of the death culture will crumble the nations so that they can be rebuilt in truth and life.

The movement in my heart and the movements in the hearts of many around the world are guided by the Holy Spirit and will not make sense to those guided by "news" coverage, cultural opinions, power-hungry leaders, personal reputation, fear, or emotionally abusive parents. Let's keep moving in faith as the Holy Spirit leads and not stop to seek out the approval of humans – not a teacher, pastor or mother. The approval of any human will not be my plumb line, my measuring stick. No, the Word of God is. The Word of God is the lens I will interpret my God given dreams

Authority To Be You

In Christ, I have the authority and freedom to be completely ME in every circumstance and situation. I do not need my mother's permission to be ME! We do not need our mother's validation, support or love. Nope! None of it! She is free to live her own life however she chooses. We are free from every expectation they ever had of us. You and I were created for a powerful purpose by the Almighty God. Our purpose is to glorify God, not our mother or anybody else.

My mother did not know my purpose, nor how powerful my purpose is. In all honesty, I do not believe my mother knows her own purpose or that she was created with a powerful purpose to glorify God herself. If she was truly in tune with her own purpose I would have a different story and would be writing a different book. But what I can do is pray for my mother to go on her own healing journey so she can fulfill her God-ordained purpose.

God Fights For Me

When I realized it was one sided, I was the only one who wanted a healthy mother daughter relationship and was the only one fighting for it, I was done. I walked away. A piece of my heart ached with the hope she would realize I am worth fighting for and come after me. The larger part of me knew hanging onto that hope would result in further pain. She has not fought for me.

But this realization deepened my understanding about my relationship with the Lord. I didn't need my mother to fight for me. Jesus has fought for me and has continued to fight for me every time I stray away. He truly wants all of me, and when He has all of me that is when I will fully be free. Longing for a person to fight for me is bondage. Giving myself completely to the One who has and will continue to fight for me is freedom.

Taking Ownership Of My Breakthrough And Freedom

Even though I could blame my parents for the way I ended up I cannot allow their mistakes to determine my future. I cannot blame them for who I will be tomorrow. I'm grown; what I do with each moment is my choice. At one time it was their fault, but NOT anymore. I invite the Spirit of breakthrough into my life, I ask for fresh wisdom daily and I walk with Wisdom. I continually engage in my relationship with my Heavenly Father so I will not lose the ground I have gained.

Give Thanks!

God is so good! I cannot go on without praising the Lord for what He has done. He has healed my heart, He has led me into belonging and identity, He is guiding me into my destiny and works through me to multiply His Kingdom. Previously my mind naturally wanted to focus on the negative as a defense mechanism to protect my wounded heart. Now that my heart is healed I naturally want to see the good, exciting work God is doing. Rather than focusing on the negative I focus on what I can be thankful for. My thankful heart melts the negativity and clears my vision to see what the Lord is doing.

I saw a meme on Facebook once that said, "Happy People Aren't Thankful, Thankful People Are Happy." In the Bible I read, "In everything **give thanks**; for this is the will of God in Christ Jesus for you" (1 Thess. 5:18 NKJV). Giving thanks is such a beautiful habit. I desire to give God praise and thanksgiving all day. I want to show my appreciation, and in doing so I strengthen my bond with my Heavenly Father.

A great gratitude activity I have done is make a list of the things I love in my life and love about myself. Keep a list like this in a place where you can easily access it. Whenever you have a tough or challenging day look over the list and praise the Lord for every one of the items listed. A thankful heart shifts our mindset to look at the world through God's eyes and not our own. I have found it makes a huge difference to not just give thanks in my head, but to say it out loud.

Things I Love About Me (in no particular order)

1) I love that I am adventurous; I feel I was born for it, to seek it out and experience the fullness of it.
2) I love experiencing new things, going to new places and trying new foods.
3) I love that I am not super skilled in any one area. I know a little bit about a whole lot of stuff. I think if I focused on one area, I would be bored.
4) I love that my love language is acts of service. I feel so loved when people help me with things especially when I am feeling overwhelmed by a large load of whatever. And I am also often the first to volunteer to help out with…whatever.
5) I love clear directions and instructions especially with new things I have never done before. I do not read minds well. Absolutely not my forte.
6) I love that I grew up in British Columbia. After traveling the world I am convinced that I grew up in the most beautiful place on earth, and I am so thankful.
7) I love that I have such a zest for life. I want to experience everything life has to offer me. Routine and staying settled is miserable for me, at least it has been so far.
8) I love that I have a glass-half-full outlook on life.
9) I love that I love to play; you can find me climbing the jungle gyms with my kiddos at the playground – my favorite is the swings. Playing dress-up is also a favorite with my kiddos.
10) I love that I have a curiosity for new information. I am the person who wants to read every plaque, pamphlet and information board at a museum.

11) I love that I am imaginative and creative.
12) I love telling stories from my life experiences; some things I just can't make up.
13) I love that I have a little bit of a competitive side. A little friendly competition is actually quite bonding.
14) I love that I am a visionary. I love coming up with new ideas, new ways of doing things and new experiences I could have.
15) I love that I am extremely flexible, and I don't mean physically. I can go with the flow like a champ. I can easily adapt to new environments, schedules and projects.
16) I love that I am free spirited, I have a little wild in me.
17) I love that I am spontaneous. It is hard for me to plan a vacation, but super easy for me to jump in the car at a moment's notice for a road trip.
18) I love that I am loyal. When I commit to a relationship, project or job I take my commitment seriously.
19) I love that I like to do things *just for fun* and maybe just to say I've done it. You know, bragging rights…
20) I love that I love nachos – a good platter of loaded nachos with lots of olives, mushrooms, salsa and guacamole- maybe my second love language.
21) I love that I love connecting with a kindred spirit.
22) I love my love for the ocean, forests and mountains. I am mesmerized by the beauty of these creations.
23) I love that I love spending time with my Heavenly Father, however that may look; jumping, shouting, hands lifted high, flag waving, dancing, on my knees, flat on my face, sitting, walking, or conversing in a mundane activity.
24) I love my voice and I am not afraid to use it. I love using my voice for teaching and equipping the saints for advancing the Kingdom of God. Seriously, I love the microphone.
25) I love the energy of a really good celebration.
26) I love that I am a passionate person.
27) I love that I am a hard worker.

28) I love my sense of style. I like being a tad bit hippy.

29) I love that I am not afraid to make mistakes, because I know that my mistakes do not define me.

30) I love my unboxed heart. There is so much more to explore; the depth of who God created me to be will have me exploring and learning for my whole earthly life and beyond.

I Will Never Give Up On Me

My Heavenly Father has never and will never give up on me. I choose to not get discouraged when I do not see the results I desire in the timeframe I want. God is in control. His timing is perfect even if it doesn't feel like it at the time. He sees the bigger picture. I choose to trust in Him and keep fighting the good fight.

"Fight the good fight of the faith [in the conflict with evil]; take hold of the eternal life to which you were called, and [for which] you made the good confession [of faith] in the presence of many witnesses." 1 Timothy 6:12 (AMP)

When I feel stuck I try to remember to ask myself if I am being obedient to His Word. As you know God asked me to write this book more than ten years ago, and I spent those ten years feeling incredibly stuck. Then, the Lord revealed to me that I felt stuck because I wasn't obedient. A great question to ask ourselves every day is, "What is it the Lord is asking me to do?" Often what He is asking us to do is something we don't feel like doing or it feels too hard. I have learned that if I want the big results I have to do the things I don't feel like doing. I have to do what I don't want to do. God will not honor lazy.

Box Of Gold

Finally, I want to end with a picture the Lord gave me. When I was positioning my heart to be aligned with God's I went on a mass heart cleaning spree, tackling all the storage places of my heart. I went through box after box finding all kinds of junk I had collected over the years. Some of the junk I didn't know was there, some of the junk I forgot was there and some of the junk I knew was there but struggled to part with it. I had to make the difficult decision and commitment to throw out everything God led me to.

As my mass cleaning cleared up significant space in my heart I was able to see a box hidden away and forgotten about. In my vision I saw myself grab this hidden box. I could tell this box had been there a long time. It was covered in layers of dust. There was something different about this box compared to the others. It was somehow much lighter and had a different feel to it.

I was drawn to it and anticipation swelled up inside of me. Curious about its contents, I slowly opened the box and was almost blinded by the glow of what was inside. It was a box full of gold. In that moment I questioned the Lord, "Gold?" I was confused. Why was a box of gold in my heart's storage among all the trash I had been pitching? The Lord replied, "Yes, that box is YOU. The true you got packed up and stored away a long time ago. My daughter, do not hide in the basement of your heart anymore. You were made to be beautiful. You were made pure. You were made to be creative, to solve problems and to strategize with Heaven. You are a gift to the world. You were made to shine. You were made to be seen. You were made to be heard. It is time; unbox your heart."

Unboxed Prayer

Dear Father,

Thank you for making me exactly as You did. Guide me, show me and lead me to be everything and do everything You already planned for me to do. Help me to love every bit of me the way You do. I never want to go back to the way I was. I pray that I keep growing and learning who You are, who I am and who I am in You. Lead me to be Your voice, speaking truth and bringing clarity wherever I go. I want to be Your mouth piece, I want to be Your messenger. Fill me with Your Holy Spirit and only let Your words come out. Anything I say or do that is not of You, I pray it will never have any growth, die and be forgotten. Anoint me to be Your speaker of truth, setting people free from the bondages of their past. Thank you for creating this desire in me. I know You did not create me the way You did to make me feel weirdly alone; You have a mighty, powerful purpose for me to see hearts set free and people step into their true identity, equipped to take territory for the Kingdom. Bless me, expand my territory, keep me from the evil one and be glorified.

In the mighty name of Yeshua, AMEN!

About the Author

Kari L. Jones, a passionate lover of Jesus, is madly in love with her husband and four children. Adventuring, traveling, exploring and discovering new places and things with her family fills her joy cup.

Kari is a passionate teacher with a deep desire to equip God's children to advance the Kingdom, draw others closer to the Father's heart and glorify His name. She strongly believes that every person is created for a unique and powerful purpose and has a strong, impactful, solution-bringing movement inside of them waiting to be ignited for the Kingdom here on earth. Kari gets excited about seeing people become empowered to be and accomplish what they were made for.

Learn more now at **www.KariLJones.com**

For interview and speaking requests and to submit reader testimonials, please contact Kari now at **kari@kariljones.com**

kariljones.com

Get updates and connect with Kari on Facebook at her Kari L. Jones author page:

https://bit.ly/3Dh6nYq

www.ingramcontent.com/pod-product-compliance
Lightning Source LLC
Chambersburg PA
CBHW071418090426
42737CB00011B/1505